M000073662

THE
MANCHESTER
UNITED
SUPPORTER'S
BOOK

First published in 2011
Second edition published in 2017

Copyright © Carlton Books Limited 2011, 2017

Carlton Books Limited
20 Mortimer Street
London W1T 3JW

A CIP catalogue record for this book is available from the British Library

ISBN 978-1-78097-986-1

Editor: Martin Corteel
Project art editor: Luke Griffin
Production: Lisa Cook

Printed and bound by
CPI Group (UK) Ltd,
Croydon, CRO 4YY

INDEPENDENT AND UNOFFICIAL

THE
MANCHESTER
UNITED
SUPPORTER'S
BOOK

SECOND EDITION

JOHN WHITE

CARLTON
BOOKS

The publishers would like to thank the following sources for their kind permission to reproduce the pictures in the plate section of this book.

Picture Quiz 1: (A) Empics Sport/PA Images; (B) Bob Thomas/Popperfoto/ Getty Images; (C) John Chillingworth/Getty Images; (D) Neal Simpson/Press Association Images

Picture Quiz 2: (A) PA Images; (B) Mike Marsland/WireImage/Getty Images; (C) Tullio M Puglia/Getty Images; (D) Dave Hogan/Getty Images

Picture Quiz 3: (A) VI-Images/Getty Images; (B) Getty Images; (C) Hulton Archive/Getty Images; (D) Manchester Daily Express/Getty Images

Picture Quiz 4: (A & D) Bob Thomas/Getty Images; (B) VI-Images; (C) Ben Radford/Getty Images

Picture Quiz 5: (A & C) Everett/REX/Shutterstock; (B) Sipa Press/REX/ Shutterstock; (D) ©ARP/Everett/REX/Shutterstock

Picture Quiz 6: (A) Philippe Lopez/AFP/Getty Images; (B) Craig Mercer/ CameraSport/Getty Images; (C) Foto Olimpik/NurPhoto/Getty Images; (D) TF-Images/Getty Images

Picture Quiz 7: (A) IMG Stock Studio/Shutterstock; (B) Comstock Images/Getty Images; (C) Dorling Kindersley/Getty Images; (D) John Foxx/Getty Images

Picture Quiz 8: (A) Bob Thomas/Getty Images; (B) Getty Images; (C) David Cannon/Getty Images; (D) Stanley Chou/Getty Images

Every effort has been made to acknowledge correctly and contact the source and/or copyright holder of each picture and Carlton Books Limited apologises for any unintentional errors or omissions that will be corrected in future editions of this book.

CONTENTS

Dedication

I would like to dedicate this book to all of my fellow United fans but especially: Adrian & Andrew Abbott, Stuart & David Anderson, Marshall Angus, David & David Jnr. Bailie, Kevin Banks, Michael (aka Levi) Bellamy, Gerard Bennett, Stephen Black, Jean & George Buchanan, Davey Campbell, Ryan Clark (my nephew), Bill Clarkson, Gerard Clifton, Mark Connolly, Kate & Nathan Crangle, Pat Crerand, Geordie Crossett, Lana Crossey, Anne Cullen, Robert & Mark Dallas, Addy, Andrew & Rachel Dearnaley, John & Martin Dempsey, Colm & Michael Devine, Frankie Dodds, Gerard Farrell, Vicky Fisher, Gerry & Shane Fitzpatrick, Martin Fox, Damien, Patricia and Nicole Friel, Davy Fulton, Mark & Raymond Gibson, Harry & John Gregg, Mike Hartley, Gerry Hastings, Johnny Hero, Jim, Chris, Ciaran, James & Lauren Hetherington, Eamonn Holmes, Billy, Betty & Mark Irvine, Alan Keegan, Damien Kerr, Jim & Jim Kyle Jnr, Matthew Leydon, Dessie & Jack Lindsay, Marcus Logue, Neilly & Ryan McAllister, Iain McCartney, Jason, Marsha & Jack McConnell, Danny McDonald, Dylan McDonnell, John McGettrick, David McGinnity, Kieran McGrandles, Steve McGregor, Wilf McGuinness, Seamus McHugh, Niall McIvor, Aidan McKenna, Brendan McLoughlin, Malachy & Teresa McMahon, Stevie McMenemy, Scott McMillen, Donna, Fiona, Claire, Niamh & Ruth McWilliams (my mother-in-law), Damien Mahon, Stephen and Jordan Mallet, Mervyn Mawhinney, Paul Miskimmon, Kieran Moloney, Mickey & Pat Morrison, William Morrow, Lynsey Mowbray, Scott Murdock, Connolly O'Connor & Connolly Jnr, Pat O'Neill, Philip O'Neill, Stephen & Mark Perry, Bertie Pollock, Robbie Robinson, Tim Robson, Dessie & Marty Roche, Roland Sarkozi, Matthew Scharfenberg, Mervyn & Darren Shaw, Kevin & Eoin Shiels, Kieran Smyth, Manus & Sean Smyth, Charlie, Katrina and Aaron Sterrett, Alan, Andrew & Daniel Stewart, Sammy Stewart, Heather Torrens, Danielle & Paris White (my sister and niece), Rosaleen White (my mum), Danny Young and, of course, to my wife, Janice, and our two sons, Marc & Paul.

Introduction

Welcome to my *Manchester United Supporter's Book*. As you turn the pages, you turn back time to learn about the highs and lows of the world's greatest football club, Manchester United. However, this is not a history book, or a facts book, or a trivia book or indeed a stats book; instead it is a fascinating mixture of all of these ingredients. As you go through the various entries, you will be taken on a magical journey unveiling various events from the club's birth in 1878 to the end of the 2016–17 season, which have contributed to the mystique surrounding the most successful club in English football history. From humble railway workers to Wayne Rooney and some magnificent players in between, including United's Trinity of Sir Bobby Charlton, Denis Law and George Best, this book is crammed with stories about many players who have worn the red of United with pride.

I love researching the history of Manchester United and I always seem to learn something new, which excites me. You will see that I have listed many quirky facts about United, covering the odd, bizarre, unbelievable and sometimes truly outrageous, which I hope my fellow Reds will enjoy. There is no other club in the world which attracts the same appeal, fascination, history and loyal support that Manchester United does. So as you read this book on the bus going to or from work, browse through it in an airport as you wait to catch a flight or lie on your back soaking up the rays on holiday, just remember that everyone will know that you are a Red.

In closing, I really do hope that the *Manchester United Supporter's Book* gives you as much pleasure to read as it gave me to compile. Let's hope that the players we have today can help extend the success of our club on the pitch and continue to win trophies leaving the others in the shade. Believe!

John White
June 2017

CHAPTER

1

MANCHESTER UNITED FACTS & TRIVIA

Being a Manchester United fan is great fun. Some of the world's greatest footballers and coaches have plied their trade for the world's greatest club and appeared at one of the most iconic sporting venues on the planet. And with these superstars come some fantastic and fascinating stories.

Over the next few pages you will learn about the great characters who have graced Old Trafford, the famous games, funny stories, historic events, all in bite-sized chunks. From legends such as Sir Bobby Charlton and Ryan Giggs to those who didn't quite make the grade, see Nick Culkin, there is an endless supply of titbits to amuse and amaze.

For those of you who love lists and statistics, there is plenty in this section. On almost every other page there is a list of some description, be it records such as appearances and goalscorers, or the more obscure – player autobiographies, superstar supporters and television advertisements. The beauty of this chapter, in fact the whole book, is that you don't have to read it from beginning to end; you can dip in and out as you wish.

A bit like a giant buffet, you are sure to find more than a few things that you like, but you will probably want to sample a little bit of everything.

Managers since 1903

Dates	Name
1903–12	**Ernest Mangnall**
1912–13	**JJ Bentley***
1914–21	**John Robson**
1921–26	**John Chapman**
1926–27	**Clarence Hilditch****
1927–31	**Herbert Bamlett**
1931–32	**Walter Crickmer**
1932–37	**Scott Duncan**
1937–45	**Walter Crickmer**
1945–69	**Sir Matt Busby**
1969–70	**Wilf McGuinness**
1970–71	**Sir Matt Busby**
1971–72	**Frank O'Farrell**
1972–77	**Tommy Docherty**
1977–81	**Dave Sexton**
1981–86	**Ron Atkinson**
1986–2013	**Sir Alex Ferguson**
2013–14	**David Moyes**
2014–2016	**Louis van Gaal**
2016 to date	**Jose Mourinho**

*Club Secretary – responsible for team selection **Player–manager*

Old Trafford Museum Heroes

Four players have individual exhibitions at the Manchester United Museum, blending a state-of-the-art interactive experience with historical exhibits: Sir Bobby Charlton, Ryan Giggs, Denis Law and Wayne Rooney.

Keeping it tight at the back

When Nottingham Forest's Stan Collymore scored in the 65th minute at Old Trafford on 17 December 1994, his strike was the first Premier League goal that United had conceded at home in 1,133 minutes of play. United lost 2–1.

Bombs fall on Old Trafford

On the night of 11 March 1941 Old Trafford was virtually demolished as Hitler's bombers targeted the vast Trafford Park industrial complex in an attempt to halt engineering production for Britain's war effort. Only three days earlier, on the 8th, Manchester United had played what proved to be their last game at Old Trafford for quite some time, beating Bury 7–3 (Carey 3, Rowley 3, Smith). After the bombing, United filed a claim with the War Damage Commission for reconstruction of the ground and were awarded £22,278. Meanwhile, the club had to rent Maine Road from their City neighbours, for around £5000 a year plus a percentage of the gate receipts, until Old Trafford could be rebuilt – a process that took eight years.

All over in 12 seconds

Nick Culkin's debut in goal for Manchester United was as a sub at Arsenal on 22 August 1999. The referee blew for full-time 12 seconds later. It was Culkin's only first-team game.

United's historical league status

Seasons	League/Division
1888–89	Football Combination
1889–92	Football Alliance
1892–94	Division One
1894–1906	Division Two
1906–15	Division One
1915–19	Wartime League (Lancashire Section)
1919–22	Division One
1922–25	Division Two
1925–31	Division One
1931–36	Division Two
1936–37	Division One
1937–38	Division Two
1938–39	Division One
1939–40	Wartime Regional League (Western Division)
1940–46	Wartime Football League (Northern Section)
1946–74	Division One
1974–75	Division Two
1975–92	Division One
1992 to date	Premier League

Proud home record falls

When Fenerbahce beat Manchester United at Old Trafford in the UEFA Champions League on 30 October 1996, they took United's 40-year, 57-game unbeaten home European record. The 1–0 reverse also meant that United had failed to score for the first time in 27 home games in the European Cup.

Immortal Lawman

On 23 February 2002 Manchester United legend Denis Law celebrated his immortality at Old Trafford when he unveiled a 10-foot-tall statue of himself at the Stretford End. The statue was commissioned by Manchester United from sculptor Ben Panting. Said Denis during the ceremony, "I'm very glad to be here doing this. And I hope my family are happy I'm here too, because usually when you unveil a statue it's when the person is no longer around. This would truly be a great honour for any footballer but it is especially so for me to be back in the Stretford End where the fans will always hold a special place in my heart." Later that day Manchester United beat Aston Villa 1–0 at Old Trafford in the Premier League thanks to a Ruud van Nistelrooy goal.

Defiant European pioneers

On 12 September 1956 United defied FA orders and participated in their first ever European competition fixture. United played Anderlecht in Belgium in the preliminary round (first leg) of the European Cup. The Reds won the game 2–0 in front of 35,000 people with goals from Viollet and Taylor.

Sparky's 100th wins title for United

Mark Hughes scored his 100th League goal for United in a 2–0 win over Crystal Palace at Selhurst Park on 21 April 1993. It effectively won the Reds their first Premier League title.

Glittering prizes

Premier League champions (record 13 occasions)
1993, 1994, 1996, 1997, 1999, 2000, 2001, 2003, 2007, 2008,
2009, 2011, 2013
Runners-up: 1995, 1998, 2006, 2010

FA Cup winners (12 occasions) 1909, 1948, 1963, 1977, 1983,
1985, 1990, 1994, 1996, 1999, 2004, 2016
Runners-up: 1957, 1958, 1976, 1979, 1995, 2005, 2007

European Cup/Champions League winners (3 occasions)
1968, 1999, 2008; Runners-up: 2009, 2011

European Cup Winners' Cup winners (1 occasion) 1991

UEFA Europa League winners (1 occasion) 2017

UEFA Super Cup winners (1 occasion) 1991
Runners-up: 1999, 2008

Intercontinental Cup winners (2 occasions) 1999, 2008
Runners-up: 1968

League Division One champions (7 occasions)
1908, 1911, 1952, 1956, 1957, 1965, 1967
Runners-up: 1947, 1948, 1951, 1959, 1964, 1968, 1980, 1988, 1992

League Division Two champions (2 occasions) 1936, 1975

League Cup winners (5 occasions) 1992, 2006, 2009, 2010,
2017; Runners-up: 1983, 1991, 1994, 2003

FA Charity / Community Shield winners (17 occasions)
1908, 1911, 1952, 1956, 1957, 1983, 1993, 1994, 1996, 1997,
2003, 2007, 2008, 2010, 2011, 2013, 2016
Joint-winners: 1965, 1967, 1977, 1990
Runners-up: 1948, 1963, 1985, 1998, 1999, 2000, 2001, 2004, 2009

Friends and Foes

Louis van Gaal, Manchester United manager 2014–16, coached Barcelona from 1997 to 2000. At Camp Nou, van Gaal's assistant was Jose Mourinho, his successor as United boss in 2016. They occupied opposite dugouts in the 2010 UEFA Champions League Final, when Mourinho's Inter Milan beat van Gaal's Bayern Munich 2–0 in Madrid.

The Sir Bobby Charlton Stand

On 3 April 2016, Old Trafford's South Stand was renamed the Sir Bobby Charlton Stand in honour of the United legend who scored 249 goals in 758 appearances, 1956–73.

Pre-league football

Before the start of the 1888–89 season Newton Heath applied to join the Football League. Their application received just one vote and was rejected. The Heathens joined forces with other disappointed applicants and formed a new, "unofficial" league, the Football Combination. Newton Heath won the League title in its only season before it was wound up in April 1889 and the balance of League funds were donated to a Derby orphanage. Newton Heath, together with many other teams from the Combination, then became founder members of the Football Alliance. The Heathens played three seasons of Alliance football, their best finish being as runners-up in 1891–92.

The captains' log

The following players have all captained Manchester United:

Harry Stafford	Maurice Setters	Steve Bruce
Jack Peddie	Noel Cantwell	Brian McClair
Charlie Roberts	David Herd	Paul Ince
George Stacey	Pat Crerand	Gary Pallister
George Hunter	Denis Law	Mike Phelan
Frank Barson	John Connelly	Neil Webb
Hugh McLenahan	Willie Morgan	Eric Cantona
Louis Page	Ian Ure	Peter Schmeichel
Jimmy Brown	Martin Buchan	Roy Keane
Johnny Carey	Sammy McIlroy	Ryan Giggs
Stan Pearson	George Graham	Gary Neville
Jack Warner	Lou Macari	Nicky Butt
Allenby Chilton	Brian Greenhoff	Ruud van Nistelrooy
Charlie Mitten	Stewart Houston	Phil Neville
Ray Wood	Arthur Albiston	Rio Ferdinand
Johnny Berry	Steve Coppell	Cristiano Ronaldo
Roger Byrne	Kevin Moran	Nemanja Vidic
Bill Foulkes	Ray Wilkins	Robin van Persie
Dennis Viollet	Mike Duxbury	Michael Carrick
Bobby Charlton	Bryan Robson	Chris Smalling
Albert Quixall	Frank Stapleton	Juan Mata
Ernie Taylor	Norman Whiteside	Wayne Rooney

Lal Hilditch bows out

On 30 January 1932 Clarence "Lal" Hilditch played his last game for United in a 3–2 win over Nottingham Forest at Old Trafford. Hilditch spent 16 seasons at Old Trafford and was the only player-manager in the history of the club. He was in charge 1926–27.

Beaten by underdogs

Manchester United have lost two Wembley finals to teams from a lower division. In the 1976 FA Cup final they were beaten by Southampton from Division Two; in 1991 they lost in the League Cup final to Sheffield Wednesday, also from Division Two.

The outcasts

At the end of the 1907–08 season, when Manchester United were crowned League champions for the first time in their history, many of the club's players were the target of the football authorities for having played a role in the formation of the Players' Union. In 1908 the players threatened to strike and ended up having to train at nearby Fallowfield; they named themselves "The Outcasts". However, a strike was avoided when the Football Association and the Football League decided to recognize the Players' Union prior to the start of the 1908–09 season.

Unlucky Ibra

Zlatan Ibrahimovic has played for six UEFA Champions League winners: Ajax Amsterdam, Juventus, Inter Milan, Barcelona, AC Milan and Manchester United. However, it is the one trophy that has eluded him in a glittering career.

Centurion goalscorers

All competitive games up to the end of the 2016–17 season

Player	Number of goals
Wayne **Rooney**	253
Bobby **Charlton**	249
Denis **Law**	237
Jack **Rowley**	211
Dennis **Viollet**	179
George **Best**	179
Ryan **Giggs**	168
Joe **Spence**	168
Mark **Hughes**	163
Paul **Scholes**	155
Ruud **van Nistelrooy**	150
Stan **Pearson**	148
David **Herd**	145
Tommy **Taylor**	131
Brian **McClair**	127
Ole Gunnar **Solskjaer**	126
Andrew **Cole**	121
Cristiano **Ronaldo**	117
Sandy **Turnbull**	101
Joe **Cassidy**	100
George **Wall**	100

Master Ferguson

On 8 October 1997 Alex Ferguson was awarded an Honorary Master of Arts Degree by Manchester University.

Hey Big Spenders

Prior to the start of the 2016–17 season, Manchester United broke the world record transfer fee when they paid £89.3m to Juventus for Paul Pogba. United then took their spending beyond the £100m mark when they brought Henrikh Mkhitaryan to Old Trafford from Borussia Dortmund for £26m for a total spend of £115.3m. Pogba's fee broke the previous world record transfer fee of £86m, paid by Real Madrid to Tottenham Hotspur in 2013 for Gareth Bale.

Giggsy the boss

When Manchester United manager David Moyes was sacked on 22 April 2014, Ryan Giggs was appointed caretaker player-manager. The United legend took charge of four games, winning two, drawing and losing one each. Three months later, United appointed Louis van Gaal as the club's new manager after the Dutchman led the Netherlands to the semi-finals of the 2014 Fifa World Cup in Brazil.

Puskas almost joined United

Shortly after the Munich Air Disaster the great Hungarian striker Ferenc Puskas offered to join United to help their rebuilding programme following the deaths of eight first-team players. However, Puskas could not speak English and the proposed move never materialized.

Reds in the book

Usually with ghostly assistance, many United notables have penned their memoirs. With no intended comment on their respective literary merits, Cantona On Cantona, Keane and other self-explanatory book titles have been omitted from this list.

Title	Author (Year)
After the Ball	**Nobby Stiles** (2003)
Back from the Brink	**Paul McGrath** (2007)
Behind the Dream	**Joe Jordan** (2005)
Big Ron: A Different Ball Game	**Ron Atkinson** (1999)
Blessed	**George Best** (2001)
Born to Score	**Dwight Yorke** (2010)
Call the Doc	**Tommy Docherty** (1981)
Determined: The Autobiography	**Norman Whiteside** (2008)
Father of Football	**Sir Matt Busby** (1994)
First Among Unequals	**Viv Anderson** (2010)
For Club and Country	**Gary & Phil Neville** (1998)
Forward for England	**Bobby Charlton** (1967)
Frankly Speaking	**Frank Stapleton** (1991)
Harry's Game	**Harry Gregg** (2002)
Head to Head	**Jaap Stam** (2002)
Heading for Victory	**Steve Bruce** (1994)
Living for Kicks	**Denis Law** (1963)
Managing My Life	**Alex Ferguson** (2001)
Moments	**Cristiano Ronaldo** (2007)
My Idea of Fun	**Lee Sharpe** (2006)
My Manchester United Years	**Sir Bobby Charlton** (2007)
My Memories of Manchester United	**Norman Whiteside** (2003)
My Side	**David Beckham** (2003)
My Story So Far	**Wayne Rooney** (2006)
Never Turn the Other Cheek	**Pat Crerand** (2007)
Odd Man Out	**Brian McClair** (1997)
On a Wing and a Prayer	**Steve Coppell** (2009)
Soccer at the Top	**Sir Matt Busby** (1974)
The Lawman	**Denis Law** (2001)
The Red Dragon	**Mark Hughes** (1994)
Tooting Common to the Stretford End	**Alex Stepney** (2010)
Un Reve Modeste et Fou	**Eric Cantona** (1993)
United I Stand	**Bryan Robson** (1984)
United We Stand	**Noel Cantwell** (1965)
We Shall Not Be Moved	**Lou Macari** (1976)
Will To Win, A	**Alex Ferguson** (1997)

Three games, three goalkeepers

On Christmas Day 1902 Herbert Birchenough played in goal for United in a 1–1 draw with Manchester City in Division Two. On Boxing Day Birchenough was replaced in goal by James Whitehouse for the 2–2 draw with Blackpool. The following day United used their third goalkeeper in three successive League games over three consecutive days when James Saunders was put in goal for the 2–1 win over Barnsley. All three matches were played at Clayton.

Two games, two cup finals

When Les Sealey replaced the suspended Peter Schmeichel in goal for United's 1994 Coca-Cola Cup final clash with Aston Villa at Wembley, it was only his second start for the team in three years. His previous start had been in the 1991 European Cup Winners' Cup final.

United's Second Home

Manchester United have won the FA Charity/Community Shield on a record 17 occasions (they have also shared four), the 17th coming with a 2–1 victory over Leicester on 17 August 2016. United also hold the record for most consecutive FA Charity/Community Shield appearances, six, between 1996 and 2001. In all, with 29, Manchester United lead the way with FA Charity/Community Shield appearances.

Old Trafford institute of management

United players who later became managers (selected teams):

Player	Team managed	Player	Team managed
Trevor Anderson	Linfield, Northern Ireland	Joe Jordan	Bristol City, Hearts Stoke City
Frank Barson	Hartlepool United	Roy Keane	Sunderland, Ipswich
William Behan	Drumcondra, Ireland	Brian Kidd	Blackburn Rovers
Shay Brennan	Waterford, Ireland	Lou Macari	West Ham, Swindon Town
Steve Bruce	Birmingham City, Wigan Athletic Sunderland, Aston Villa	Neil McBain	Ayr United
		Jim McCalliog	Halifax Town
Martin Buchan	Burnley	Wilf McGuinness	Manchester United
Francis Burns	Italia FC, Australia	Sammy McIlroy	Macclesfield N Ireland, Morecambe
		George McLachlan	Queen of the South
Noel Cantwell	Coventry City	Gordon McQueen	Airdrieonians
Johnny Carey	Blackburn Rovers	Charlie Mitten	Newcastle United
Bobby Charlton	Preston North End	Kenny Morgans	Cwmbran Town*
Allenby Chilton	Grimsby Town*	Jimmy Nicholl	Raith Rovers,* Millwall, Cowdenbeath
Steve Coppell	Crystal Palace, Reading, Brighton, Bristol C	Andy Ritchie	Oldham, Barnsley, Huddersfield
Pat Crerand	Northampton Town		
Peter Davenport	Bangor City	Bryan Robson	Middlesbrough, West Brom, Sheffield United, Thailand
Tony Dunne	Stenjker, Norway		
Darren Ferguson	Peterboro', Preston	Alex Stepney	Altrincham
Bill Foulkes	Viking Stavanger, Norway	Ole Gunnar Solskjaer	Molde FK
		Nobby Stiles	Preston North End
Johnny Giles	West Bromwich Albion	Ian Storey-Moore	Shepshed Charterhouse
George Graham	Arsenal, Tottenham		
Harry Gregg	Carlisle United	Gordon Strachan	Coventry, Southampton, Celtic Middlesbrough, Scotland
David Herd	Lincoln City		
Clarence "Lal" Hilditch	Manchester United*	Chris Turner	Hartlepool United
Gordon Hill	Northwich Victoria	Dennis Viollet	Crewe Alexandra
Mark Hughes	Blackburn Rovers, Wales, Man City, Fulham, Stoke City	Ray Wilkins	QPR*, Fulham
		Walter Winterbottom	England
Paul Ince	Macclesfield T, MK Dons., Blackburn R, Notts County		

Player-manager.

Follow my leader

Bastian Schweinsteiger spent 13 seasons in Bayern Munich's first team, 2002–15, winning almost every available trophy. His manager from 2009–11, Louis van Gaal, admired his qualities so much that he signed him for Manchester United in 2015.

The world's most valuable club

On 7 June 2017, Manchester United replaced Real Madrid as the world's most valuable football team, according to *Forbes* magazine. The club were valued at $3.69bn (£2.86bn) and returned to the summit of the annual Rich List for the first time since 2012. Real Madrid slipped to third place, valued at $3.58bn (£2.77bn) whilst FC Barcelona were second, valued at $3.64bn (£2.82bn). "Manchester United's return to the top spot is a testament to their powerful brand and marketing acumen," *Forbes* Media assistant managing editor, Mike Ozanian, said in a statement.

Valencia v Valencia at Old Trafford

On 6 August 2009, United beat CF Valencia 2–0 in a friendly at Old Trafford. Although he didn't score, Antonio Valencia did have the unusual experience of playing against Valencia.

Also known as

Nickname	Player	Nickname	Player
Apache	Carlos Tevez	**Judge**	Lou Macari
Baby-Faced Assassin	Ole Gunnar Solskjaer	**Keano**	Roy Keane
		King	Denis Law
Bamber	Alan Gowling	**Knocker**	Enoch West
Berry	Robert Beresford Brown	**Larry White**	Laurent Blanc
Big Al	Alex Stepney	**Le King**	Eric Cantona
Billy	Liam Whelan	**Little Pea (Chicarito)**	Javier Hernandez
Black Pearl of Inchicore	Paul McGrath	**Merlin**	Gordon Hill
Black Prince	Alex Dawson	**Mr Soccer**	Joe Spence
Bogota Bandit	Charlie Mitten	**Pancho**	Stuart Pearson
Boom Boom	Duncan Edwards	**Pocket Hercules**	Herbert Burgess
Busby	Paul Parker	**Robbo**	Bryan Robson
Cario	Johnny Carey	**Rocket Ronaldo**	Cristiano Ronaldo
Chicharito	Javier Hernandez	**Roonaldo**	Wayne Rooney
Choccy	Brian McClair	**Shark**	Joe Jordan
Cowboy	Bill Foulkes	**Sharpey**	Lee Sharpe
Daisy	Gary Pallister	**Shay**	Seamus Anthony Brennan
Dazzler	Darren Fletcher	**Smudger**	Alan Smith
Dolly	Steve Bruce	**Snake Hips**	Eddie Colman
El Beatle	George Best	**Sparky**	Mark Hughes
Fabs	Fabien Barthez	**Stroller**	George Graham
Ghost	Charlie Roberts	**Sunbed**	Clayton Blackmore
Giggsy	Ryan Giggs	**Tank**	Duncan Edwards
Gunner	Jack Rowley	**Turnbull the Terrible**	Sandy Turnbull
Happy	Nobby Stiles	**Welsh Wizard/**	
Jap	Danny Wallace	**Old Skinny**	Billy Meredith

100 points

When they defeated Oldham Athletic 5–2 at Boundary Park on 29 December 1993, Manchester United notched up a total of 100 League points for the calendar year.

Old Trafford closed by the FA

As a result of a knife-throwing incident during a League game at Old Trafford against Newcastle United on 27 February 1971, the Football Association closed Old Trafford at the start of the following season, 1971–72.

Dramatic comeback thwarted

Arsenal took the lead after only 12 minutes of the 1979 FA Cup final through Brian Talbot. Then just before the interval, Frank Stapleton scored to put the Gunners 2–0 up. The Reds were still 2–0 down with four minutes of the match remaining, and then a remarkable sequence of events unfolded. Gordon McQueen pulled a goal back for United. It seemed merely a consolation until Sammy McIlroy wove his way through the Arsenal defence to place his shot past Pat Jennings and bring the two sides level with less than a minute on the clock. But victory was snatched from United's grasp when Alan Sunderland scored for Arsenal in the dying seconds of the game.

A long season

During the 1993–94 season Manchester United played 63 first-team games: 42 Premier League games, 9 League Cup ties (including the final), 7 FA Cup ties (including the final), 4 European Cup fixtures and the FA Charity Shield.

As seen on TV

United players appearing in television commercials:

David Beckham	Adidas Predator boots	**Sir Alex Ferguson & United team**	Nike
David Beckham	Brylcreem	**Sir Alex Ferguson & United team**	UNICEF
David Beckham	Gillette Razor Blades /Shaving Gel	**Roy Keane**	Diadora
David Beckham	Pepsi	**Roy Keane**	Kit Kat
David Beckham	Police Sunglasses	**Roy Keane**	Walker's Crisps
George Best	Cookstown Sausages	**Gary & Phil Neville**	Vodafone
George Best	Egg Marketing Board	**Joe Jordan**	Heineken
George Best	Fore Aftershave	**Ruud van Nistelrooy**	Coca-Cola
George Best	Great Universal Stores	**Ruud van Nistelrooy**	Nike
George Best	Stylo Boots	**Ruud van Nistelrooy**	Stand-up, Speak-up**
George Best	Tyne-tex Anoraks		
Steve Bruce	Sure deodorant	**Ji-Sung Park**	Nike
Eric Cantona	Eurostar	**Cristiano Ronaldo**	Pepe Jeans
Eric Cantona	Nike	**Cristiano Ronaldo**	Suzuki Jeep
Sir Bobby Charlton	Kirin Beer*	**Wayne Rooney**	Coke Zero
Sir Bobby Charlton	Mastercard	**Wayne Rooney**	Powerade
Andy Cole	Reebok	**Wayne Rooney**	Nike
Ryan Giggs	Fuji Film	**Louis Saha**	Nike
Ryan Giggs	ITV Digital	**Peter Schmeichel**	Danepak Bacon
Ryan Giggs	Quorn Burgers	**Peter Schmeichel**	Reebok
Ryan Giggs	Reebok	**Peter Schmeichel**	Sugar Puffs
Rio Ferdinand	Anti-bullying campaign	**Gordon Strachan**	Barclays Bank
		Paul Scholes	Nike
Rio Ferdinand	Stand-up, Speak-up**	**Ole Gunnar Solskjaer**	Nike
		Carlos Tevez	Joga Bonito Nike
Sir Alex Ferguson	Barclays Bank	**Ray Wilkins**	Tango (voice-over)

*Shown only in Japan. **Campaign against racism.*

This Is Your Life

Prior to the Manchester Derby game at Old Trafford on 12 December 1970 Sir Matt Busby and the City manager, Joe Mercer, were presented with mementos on the pitch. Sir Matt Busby received a further surprise when Eamonn Andrews crept up on him with an invitation for a second appearance on the TV show *This Is Your Life*. United lost the game 4–1.

FA Cup football returns

On 8 January 1949 United, the FA Cup holders, played their first FA Cup fixture in ten years at Old Trafford when they thrashed Bournemouth 6–0 in front of 55,012 fans. United's previous FA Cup fixture at Old Trafford took place on 11 January 1939 when West Bromwich Albion beat them 5–1 in a third round replay.

The Sir Alex Ferguson Stand

On 5 November 2011, Old Trafford's North Stand was renamed the Sir Alex Ferguson Stand to honour his 25 years as Manchester United manager. Just over a year later, on 23 November 2012, a 9-foot (2.7 m) statue of Sir Alex, sculpted by Philip Jackson, was unveiled outside the stand. With a capacity of 26,000, it is the largest of Old Trafford's four stands and houses the Red Café and the United Museum and Trophy Room.

Celebrity Reds

Sport

Wasim Akram	cricketer
Michael Atherton	cricketer
Ainsley Bingham	boxer
Darren Campbell	athlete
Colin Croft	cricketer
Ken Doherty	snooker player
Neil Fairbrother	cricketer
Graeme McDowell	golfer
Rory McIroy	golfer
Jarkko Nieminen	tennis player
Martin Offiah	rugby player
John Virgo	snooker player
Heather Watson	tennis player

Music

Paul "Bonehead" Arthurs	guitarist
Richard Ashcroft	lead singer
Victoria Beckham	singer
Melanie Blatt	singer
Ian Brown	lead singer
Tim Burgess	lead singer
Larry Gott	guitarist
Black Grape	band
Terry Hall	lead singer
Mick Hucknall	lead singer
Kerry Katona	singer
Kym Marsh	singer
Cerys Matthews	lead singer
Morrissey	lead singer
Mani Mounfield	guitarist
Ed O'Brien	guitarist
New Order	band
John Squire	guitarist
Supergrass	band
Malcolm Treece	guitarist
Russell Watson	opera singer
Thom Yorke	lead singer

Politics

Bertie Ahern	Former Irish Prime Minister
Tony Lloyd	politician

Entertainment and media

Steven Arnold	actor
Zoe Ball	radio/TV presenter
Chris Bisson	actor
Edith Bowman	radio/TV presenter
Gordon Burns	TV presenter
Mark Chapman	sports reporter
Mark Charnock	actor
Terry Christian	TV presenter
Steve Coogan	actor
Jimmy Cricket	comedian
Angus Deayton	actor/presenter
John Dyson	TV presenter
Christopher Ecclestone	actor
Alan Halsall	actor
Eamonn Holmes	TV presenter
Ulrika Jonsson	TV personality
Patrick Kielty	comedian
Terry Kiely	actor
Mark Lamarr	radio/TV presenter
Michael Le Vell	actor
Steve McFadden	actor
Ian McShane	actor
Nemone	radio DJ
James Nesbitt	actor
Robert Powell	actor
Gary Rhodes	TV chef
Lisa Riley	actor
Shane Ritchie	actor
Jennifer Saunders	actress/comedienne
Andrew Whyment	actor
Richard Wilson	actor
Sean Wilson	actor

United's player-manager

Clarence George "Lal" Hilditch was born in Hartford, Cheshire on 2 June 1894. In October 1926, after John Chapman had been sacked, he became the first player-manager in United's history. The Reds looked to the half-back to bring back the glory days. Hilditch had joined Manchester United from Altrincham during the First World War and went on to play for United for 16 seasons, making 322 appearances. When Hilditch was appointed it was made clear to him that it was a temporary measure, but he was in charge until the end of the 1926–27 season, when Herbert Bamlett took over. Hilditch remained as a United player until he retired in 1932.

English Lion mauls the Tigers

On 23 January 2010, Wayne Rooney scored all four United goals in a 4–0 mauling of Hull City at Old Trafford. It was the first time Rooney had scored four in a professional match.

Magnificent seven for Keane

When Roy Keane captained United in the 2005 FA Cup final he set a modern day record by appearing in his seventh FA Cup final. Keane's first FA Cup final appearance was for Nottingham Forest in 1991 and he also played for United in the finals of 1994, 1995, 1996, 1999 and 2004. Lord Kinnaird played in nine of the first 11 finals in the 1870s and 1880s.

United's club record signings

Date	Player	Fee	From
1903, Jan	Alexander Bell	**£700**	Ayr Parkhouse
1904, Apr	Charlie Roberts	**£750**	Grimsby Town
1914, Mar	George Hunter	**£1300**	Chelsea
1922, Aug	Frank Barson	**£5000**	Aston Villa
1951, Aug	Johnny Berry	**£15,000**	Birmingham City
1953, Mar	Tommy Taylor	**£29,999**	Barnsley
1958, Sept	Albert Quixall	**£45,000**	Sheffield Weds
1962, July	Denis Law	**£115,000**	Torino
1972, Feb	Martin Buchan	**£120,000**	Aberdeen
1972, Mar	Ian Storey-Moore	**£200,000**	Nottingham Forest
1978, Jan	Joe Jordan	**£350,000**	Leeds United
1978, Feb	Gordon McQueen	**£495,000**	Leeds United
1979, Aug	Ray Wilkins	**£825,000**	Chelsea
1980, Oct	Garry Birtles*	**£1.25m**	Nottingham Forest
1981, Oct	Bryan Robson*	**£1.5m**	WBA
1988, July	Mark Hughes	**£1.6m**	Barcelona
1989, Aug	Gary Pallister	**£2.3m**	Middlesbrough
1989, Sept	Paul Ince	**£2.4m**	West Ham United
1993, July	Roy Keane*	**£3.75m**	Nottingham Forest
1995, Jan	Andy Cole*	**£7m**	Newcastle United
1998, July	Jaap Stam	**£10.75m**	PSV Eindhoven
1998, Aug	Dwight Yorke	**£12.6m**	Aston Villa
2001, Apr	Ruud van Nistelrooy	**£19m**	PSV Eindhoven
2002, July	Juan Sebastian Veron	**£28.1m**	SS Lazio
2002, July	Rio Ferdinand*	**£30m**	Leeds United
2008, Aug	Dimitar Berbatov	**£30.75m**	Tottenham Hotspur
2014, Jan	Juan Mata	**£37.1m**	Chelsea
2014, Aug	Angel Di Maria	**£59.7m**	Real Madrid
2016, Aug	Paul Pogba**	**£89.3m**	Juventus

British record transfer fee   **World record transfer fee*

Double not to be

Five days before the 1957 FA Cup final the Reds lifted the First Division Championship and looked set to become the first team to win the Double in the twentieth century. United's FA Cup final opponents, Aston Villa, had been the last side to do the Double. After six minutes, United goalkeeper Ray Wood collided with Villa's Peter McParland and was stretchered off, with Jackie Blanchflower going in goal. United's Double dream vanished in the second half when McParland scored twice. Tommy Taylor did pull a goal back for the Reds, and United also had what would have been a late equaliser ruled out for offside, but Villa hung on to win 2–1.

Humble beginnings

The club began life in 1878, when a group of railway workers from the Lancashire & Yorkshire Railway formed a football team and named it Newton Heath. In the early days the players changed in a nearby pub, The Three Crowns Inn, before taking the short walk to the pitch in North Road, off Monsall Road, Newton Heath.

Long service medals

Gary Neville joined Bobby Charlton, Bill Foulkes, Paul Scholes and Ryan Giggs in United's 600 games club in the 2–1 win at Stoke on 24 October 2010.

The trophy collector

Sir Alex Ferguson amassed a trophy collection that is the envy of other managers. He won 47 trophies in his managerial career with three different clubs, including 36 with Manchester United:

ST MIRREN First Division winners: 1977

ABERDEEN Premier League winners: 1980, 1984, 1985

Scottish Cup winners: 1982, 1983, 1984, 1986

League Cup winners: 1986

European Cup Winners' Cup winners: 1983

European Super Cup winners: 1983

MANCHESTER UNITED FA Cup winners: 1990, 1994, 1996, 1999, 2004

European Cup Winners' Cup winners: 1991

European Super Cup winners: 1991

League Cup winners: 1992, 2006, 2009, 2010

Premier League winners: 1993, 1994, 1996, 1997, 1999, 2000, 2001, 2003, 2007, 2008, 2009, 2011, 2013

FA Charity Shield winners: 1993, 1994, 1996, 1997 2003, 2007, 2008, 2010

European Cup winners: 1999, 2008

World Club Cup winners: 1999, 2009

Sequentially ordered

When United beat Sheffield Wednesday 3–0 at Hillsborough in the League on 7 December 1993, it was the first time since squad numbers came in that the Reds had started with players numbered 1 to 11. Roy Keane, No. 16, came on as a substitute.

Peden hat-trick for Ireland

John Peden, a Newton Heath forward in 1893–94, scored a hat-trick for Ireland against Wales in Belfast on 5 April 1893. Ireland won the game 4–3. Although English based players were not introduced into the Irish side until season 1898–99, Peden was technically a Newton Heath player when he turned out for Ireland as his registration for the Heathens was dated 23 February 1893 despite the fact that he did not play for Newton Heath until 2 September 1893.

Crowd pleasers

United kicked off the 2006–07 Premier League campaign with a scintillating 5–1 win over Fulham at Old Trafford on 20 August 2006. Following the construction of two additional sections of the stadium named The Quadrants, a new record FA Premier League crowd of 75,115 fans attended the game.

Alex is God

At the end of the 2005–06 season United's shirt sponsorship deal with Vodafone came to an end and the Reds quickly moved to sign a contract with American Insurance Group (AIG). AIG was the largest underwriter of commercial and industrial insurance in the USA. United fans were quick off the mark themselves claiming that AIG actually stood for "Alex Is God". In 2010, AIG was replaced as sponsors by Aon.

One-cap wonders

The following Manchester United players won only one full international cap for their country:

Player	Country
Francis **Burns**	Scotland
Peter **Davenport**	England
Bill **Foulkes**	England
Stewart **Houston**	Scotland
Caesar **Jenkyns**	Wales
David **Pegg**	England
Mike **Phelan**	England
Jimmy **Rimmer**	England
Alex **Stepney**	England
Ian **Storey-Moore**	England
Danny **Wallace**	England

Blues stopped in their tracks

Manchester United, the only team ever to win the Premier League title three seasons in a row – and the first to win the top division title in three consecutive years since Liverpool in the 1980s – ended Chelsea's dreams of emulating Sir Alex Ferguson's squads of 1999–2001. Chelsea went into the 2006–07 season as the reigning Premier League Champions, but it was United who claimed their ninth title, six points clear of the Blues. Having ended Chelsea's attempt at three in a row, United showed the Blues how it should be done by taking the title in 2007, 2008 and 2009 for a second hat-trick.

The first ever penalty shoot-out

United took part in the first-ever penalty shoot-out in English football. On 5 August 1970, United drew 1–1 with Hull City at Hull in the Watney Cup. The game was decided on penalties, with United progressing to the final with a 4–3 win. In the final, United were beaten 4–1 by Derby County at the Baseball Ground (scorer: Best).

United television

In August 1998 Manchester United FC launched its own television channel. MUTV broadcasts six hours a day, seven days a week from a studio at Old Trafford. The channel is available through subscription and shows live youth and reserve team games and friendlies and even FA Premier League matches.

Digs at Mrs Fullaway's

When George Best arrived in Manchester from Belfast in 1961 the club placed him in digs with a club landlady, Mrs Mary Fullaway, in Aycliffe Avenue, Chorlton-cum-Hardy, Manchester. George did not settle in Manchester in those early days he spent away from his family and even returned home to Belfast through homesickness. However, he was persuaded to return to United by Matt Busby and spent many wonderful and happy years at Mrs Fullaway's who had to contend with more than her fair share of admiring girls.

Knock them off their perch!

When Manchester United lifted the Premier League title for a 12th time in season 2010–11, their 19th League Championship, Sir Alex Ferguson lived up to his promise to United fans to knock Liverpool right off their perch by surpassing Liverpool's record haul of 18 League titles. Sir Alex added a 13th Premier League title (20th League title overall) in his final season at Old Trafford, 2012–13. When Jose Mourinho's United side beat Ajax Amsterdam 2–0 in the 2017 Europa League final, Manchester United officially became England's most successful club by winning their 45th major honour in comparison to Liverpool's haul of 44 trophies.

Liverpool: 18 League titles, 7 FA Cups, 8 League Cups, 5 European Cups/UEFA Champions League, 3 UEFA Cups and 3 European Super Cups = 44.

Manchester United: 20 League titles, 12 FA Cups, 5 League Cups, 3 European/UEFA Champions League Cups, 1 European Cup Winners' Cup, 1 UEFA Europa League, 1 European Super Cup, 1 Intercontinental Cup and 1 FIFA Club World Cup = 45.

United's Villa Park fortress

Villa Park is a favourite venue for Manchester United: since losing on the opening day of the 1995–96 season, they have not lost a Premier League match there. In the last 21 Premier League and cup meetings at Villa Park before Villa were relegated, United won 16 times and drew the other five. Their 41 Premier League points away to Villa since the 1999–2000 season is impressive, but the home return is better – 46 – 15 wins, a draw and a loss.

A Devil now in heaven

George Best died on 25 November 2005 following a long battle against liver disease. A little more than a week later, on 3 December 2005, the cities of Belfast and Manchester came to a standstill when George's funeral took place. Tens of thousands of mourners lined the streets from his home in the Cregagh estate of East Belfast to Stormont Castle to show their appreciation of his genius on the football pitch. Some people felt it was Northern Ireland's first state funeral.

Bestie's one final wish was that he hoped the people would remember him for his football. His countrymen did not disappoint him on that overcast day as fans from all walks of life said a tearful farewell to a legend. All along the funeral route fans threw flowers and scarves at the cortege as it made its way to Stormont for George's funeral service. One man in the crowd stood still, silent in his respect holding aloft a banner which summed George Best up as a footballer: "Maradona good, Pele better, George Best".

At the funeral service, hosted solemnly by fellow Northern Irishman, television and radio personality Eamonn Holmes, Brian Kennedy and Peter Corry sang songs in tribute to George whilst sporting stars, including Sir Alex Ferguson and the Manchester United team, attended the service.

On 22 May 2006, the George Best Carryduff Manchester United Supporters Club held a gala dinner in Belfast City Hall to raise monies in aid of The George Best Foundation. It was the day on which George would have celebrated his 60th birthday. The gala dinner was hosted by the Lord Mayor of Belfast and was attended by Sir Alex Ferguson, David Gill and Paddy Crerand as well as a host of other sporting stars, friends of family of the "Genius".

Top of the Pops

Manchester United have spent longer in the UK hit parade than any other football team. These are the toe-tapping songs:

Manchester United Football Club

UK, male football team vocalists (56 WEEKS)

		pos	wks
8 May 76	**Manchester United**		
	Decca F 13633	**50**	1
21 May 83	**Glory Glory Man United**		
	EMI 5390	**13**	5
18 May 85 •	**We All Follow Man United**		
	Columbia DB 9107	**10**	5
19 Jun 93	**United (We Love You)**		
	Living Beat LBECD 026	**37**	2
30 Apr 94 *	**Come On You Reds** [1]		
	PolyGram TV MANU	**2**	15
13 May 95 •	**We're Gonna Do It Again** [2]		
	PolyGram MANU 952	**6**	6
4 May 96 •	**Move Move Move (The Red Tribe)** [3]		
	Music Collection MANUCD 1	**6**	11
3 Aug 96	**Move Move Move (The Red Tribe)** [3] **(re-entry)**		
	Music Collection MANUCD 1	**50**	4
29 May 99	**Lift It High (All About Belief)** [4]		
	Music Collection MANUCD 4	**11**	6
21 Aug 99	**Lift It High (All About Belief)** [4] **(re-entry)**		
	Music Collection MANUCD 4	**75**	1

* UK No. 1 • UK Top 10

[1] Manchester United and the Champions

[2] Manchester United Football Squad featuring Stryker

[3] 1996 Manchester United FA Cup Squad

[4] 1999 Manchester United FA Cup Squad

© Guinness World Records Book of Hit Singles/The Official UK Charts Company

A hat-trick of penalties

Charlie Mitten scored three penalties for United in a 7–0 First Division home win over Aston Villa on 8 March 1950. Charlie also netted a fourth goal in the game.

Busby and Foulkes say farewell

On 15 May 1969 Sir Matt Busby managed his last European game, and Bill Foulkes played his last game in European competition, as United beat AC Milan 1–0 in the second leg of their European Cup semi-final tie at Old Trafford. Foulkes' appearance was his 52nd in Europe for the club, a record at the time. Trailing 2–0 from the first leg United pulled one goal back then, with 13 minutes remaining the Reds thought they had equalised on aggregate when Pat Crerand's cross appeared to cross the line. The goal was not given, which led to a section of the Stretford End throwing missiles onto the pitch. AC Milan's Cudicini was hit by a stone. Following this incident UEFA ordered United to erect screens behind the goals at Old Trafford for future European games, though the Reds had to wait eight years for their next match in Europe.

Seventh time lucky

When United beat Chelsea in the 2008 UEFA Champions League final, it was the first time Sir Alex Ferguson had won a penalty shoot-out (excluding the FA Charity Shield). He had lost three with Aberdeen and three with Manchester United.

England Games At Old Trafford

Date	Result
17 APRIL 1926	England 0, Scotland 1
16 NOVEMBER 1938	England 7, Northern Ireland 0
24 MAY 1997	England 2, South Africa 1
6 OCTOBER 2001	England 2, Greece 2
10 OCTOBER 2001	England 1, Sweden 1
10 SEPTEMBER 2003	England 2, Liechtenstein 0
16 NOVEMBER 2003	England 2, Denmark 3
9 OCTOBER 2004	England 2, Wales 0
26 MARCH 2005	England 4, Northern Ireland 0
8 OCTOBER 2005	England 1, Austria 0
12 OCTOBER 2005	England 2, Poland 1
30 MAY 2006	England 3, Hungary 1
3 JUNE 2006	England 6, Jamaica 0
16 AUGUST 2006	England 4, Greece 0
2 SEPTEMBER 2006	England 5, Andorra 0
7 OCTOBER 2006	England 0, FYR Macedonia 0
7 FEBRUARY 2007	England 0, Spain 1

Collection of custodians

In 1952–53 Manchester United used a club record-equalling five different goalkeepers during the season: Reg Allen, Johnny Carey, Jack Crompton, Les Olive and Ray Wood, matching the number used 57 seasons earlier. Newton Heath had used five different goalkeepers in the 1895–96 season: William Douglas, George Perrins, Joseph Ridgway, Richard Smith and Walter Whittaker.

Belfast boy on the money

On 27 November 2006, the Ulster Bank immortalized George Best with a commemorative £5 banknote. The bank issued the limited edition – there were one million of them – run of notes to commemorate the first anniversary of the death of the man voted the greatest ever Manchester United player by United fans. It depicts the Belfast Boy in both his Manchester United and Northern Ireland colours. George's father, Dickie Best, was presented with banknote number 1,000,000.

United maul Italian wolves

When AS Roma travelled to Old Trafford on 10 April 2007 holding a 2–1 lead after the first leg of their Champions League quarter-final tie, they had a confidence based on history. United had not overturned a first-leg deficit in Europe since a 1983–84 Cup-Winners Cup defeat of Barcelona. The 23-year drought was ended spectacularly as United produced an awesome display of attacking football to run out 7–1 winners on the night (8–3 on aggregate). Cristiano Ronaldo., in his 27th European game for United, scored his first two goals, and he was joined on the scoresheet by Michael Carrick (two), Alan Smith, Wayne Rooney and Patrice Evra. Carrick opened the scoring and Smith and Rooney added goals before Ronaldo netted his first as United led 4–0 half-time. Carrick and Ronaldo extended to Roma's misery before Daniele De Rossi grabbed a consolation. Evra completed the scoring.

20 famous free exits

Player	Destination and date
Zlatan **Ibrahimovic**	Released, June 2017
Darren **Fletcher**	West Bromwich Albion, February 2015
Nemanja **Vidic**	Inter Milan, July 2014
Rio **Ferdinand**	Released, July 2014
Ronny **Johnsen**	Aston Villa, June 2002
Denis **Irwin**	Wolverhampton Wanderers, June 2002
Jesper **Blomqvist**	Everton, July 2001
Teddy **Sheringham**	Tottenham Hotspur, May 2001
Jordi **Cruyff**	Alaves, July 2000
Peter **Schmeichel**	Sporting Lisbon, June 1999
Brian **McClair**	Motherwell, June 1998
Steve **Bruce**	Birmingham City, June 1996
Paul **Parker**	Released June 1996
Bryan **Robson**	Middlesbrough, May 1994
Viv **Anderson**	Sheffield Wednesday, January 1991
Kevin **Moran**	Sporting Gijon, August 1988
Martin **Buchan**	Oldham Athletic, August 1983
George **Best**	Released August 1974
Tony **Dunne**	Bolton Wanderers, August 1973
Denis **Law**	Manchester City, July 1973

Lowest ever Premier League finish

In season 2013–14, Manchester United sacked David Moyes with four League games still left to play. The club finished in seventh position, their lowest league finish since they were 13th in the old First Division in 1989–90.

The United-Liverpool rivalry

Manchester City are, of course, Manchester United's biggest rivals, attracting fans from the same city. However, in terms of competitive rivalry, there is nothing to match the one between United and Liverpool. No player has moved directly from United to Liverpool since Phil Chisnall left Old Trafford for Anfield in 1964. Indeed, in 2007 United refused Gabriel Heinze permission to join Liverpool, the defender moving to Real Madrid instead. The last player to play for both clubs was Paul Ince, who spent two years in Italy between his departure from Manchester in 1995 and his arrival on Merseyside in 2007. On the field, the clubs have met 197 times in all competitions up to May 2017. United hold a narrow advantage in the results column. This is their record:

Competition	Played	Wins	Draws	Defeats
League	168	67	46	55
FA Cup	16	9	4	3
League Cup	5	2	0	3
Other	6	1	3	2
Europa League	2	0	1	1
Total	197	78	54	65

A historic lion

Former United hero David Beckham's winning strike against Ecuador in Stuttgart on 25 June 2006 put him in the history books by becoming the only England player to have scored in three different World Cup finals (1998, 2002 and 2006).

A Ruud £1m

In June 2007, 11 months after leaving Manchester United, Ruud van Nistelrooy earned the club a £1m windfall. When United allowed the Dutch international striker to leave Old Trafford in July 2006, to join Real Madrid for £10.2m, Sir Alex Ferguson insisted on a series of clauses being put into the deal. These included a pair of £500,000 bonuses for United, one if Real Madrid won La Liga and the other if van Nistelrooy finished the season as Spain's top scorer. Madrid won the title on the final day of the season and Ruud finished the campaign with 25 goals to his name, best in La Liga.

£5m book worm

When Wayne Rooney signed the largest sports book deal in British publishing history with HarperCollins in March 2006, the young star agreed to a £5m deal, plus royalties, in return for a minimum five books to be published over a 12-year period. His first book under the deal, *Wayne Rooney, My Story So Far*, was published shortly after the 2006 World Cup Finals.

World Cup matches at Old Trafford

In the 1966 World Cup, Old Trafford provided the venue for the Pool B games of Portugal, Hungary, Bulgaria and Brazil.

Sir Alex gives Sparky a European gift

Former Old Trafford favourite Mark Hughes received a gift from Manchester United at the end of the 2005–06 season. United had qualified for the UEFA Cup as winners of the Carling Cup. But because they finished in the top two of the FA Premier League, United went into the UEFA Champions League, which opened up an extra spot for an English club in Europe's second competition, and Blackburn Rovers, managed by Hughes, were the fortunate beneficiaries.

Giggs nearly causes walk-off

When Ryan Giggs scored with a quickly-taken free kick late in United's UEFA Champions League last 16 first leg tie away to Lille on 20 February 2007 it gave the Reds a vital away goal. Lille's players were furious, especially goalkeeper Tony Sylva who protested that he was still lining-up his wall when Giggs curled the ball into the net. Sylva was booked and several Lille players looked set to walk off the pitch in protest. Play was held up for some time until they were persuaded to resume the game, which United won 1-0.

Three Lions refused

When Paul Scholes retired from international football in 2004, Sven-Goran Eriksson, Steve McClaren and Fabio Capello all tried and failed to lure him back to the national team.

Fourteen out of fourteen

In 1904–05, Manchester United won 14 consecutive League games in Division Two. The run started with a 2–0 home win over Lincoln City on 15 October 1904, ending with a 4–2 away victory at Bolton Wanderers on 3 January 1905.

Four FA cup ties in 27 days

On their way to lifting the FA Cup in 1963, as a result of the severe winter across the country, Manchester United played four rounds of the competition in 27 days, 4–30 March.

Goals aplenty

On 25 April 1959 United equalled their record total of 103 for most League goals in a season in their 2–1 away defeat at Leicester City. Warren Bradley was the United goal scorer as United ended the season First Division runners-up.

Chim-chiminey

In the 1895–96 season "Father Bird", a local chimney sweep, often entertained the Newton Heath players at his home with a supper of potato-pie or Lancashire hot-pot, liquid refreshments and a sing-song afterwards.

First name change

In the 1892–93 season the club made the decision to drop the "Lancashire & Yorkshire Railway" from their name becoming simply known as Newton Heath Football Club. The club's last game as Newton Heath Lancashire & Yorkshire Railway was against Birmingham St George's at home on 9 April 1892.

Unlucky for some

A paltry 13 spectators turned up at Old Trafford on 7 May 1921 to watch Stockport County play Leicester City in a Division Two game. The Football Association had closed County's ground for disciplinary reasons. And for the unlucky 13 that turned up the game ended scoreless.

Cup defence

When Manchester United beat Aston Villa 2–1 at Wembley Stadium to win the 2010 Carling Cup Final they became the first team to successfully defend the Football League Cup since Nottingham Forest in 1990 and only the third club in the competition's history to do so after Liverpool (1981–84 inclusive) and Forest (twice, 1979–80 and 1989–90).

Did You Know That?
United's 2010 Carling Cup success was the first time they had ever successfully defended any domestic cup.

FA Cup Final early baths

When Chris Smalling was sent off playing for Manchester United against Crystal Palace in the 2016 FA Cup Final, he became just the fourth player to be sent off in an FA Cup Final. United's Kevin Moran was the first player given his marching orders in an FA Cup Final when he was sent off against Everton in the 1985 Final (United won 1-0). Manchester City's Pablo Zabaleta (Argentina) was sent off against Wigan Athletic in the 2013 Final whilst Arsenal's Jose Antonio Reyes (Spain) saw red in the 2005 Final. Smalling was also the first Englishman sent off in an FA Cup Final. As a footnote, in the 2017 FA Cup Final between Arsenal and Chelsea, the Blues' Victor Moses became the fifth player to be dismissed – he was sent off after being shown two yellow cards.

Rocky IV look-a-like

On 5 January 2006, United signed the Serbia-Montenegro international defender Nemanja Vidic for £7 million from Spartak Moscow. Vidic began his professional career on loan at Spartak Moscow, before returning to Red Star Belgrade, and then signed permanently for Spartak in July 2004, costing the Russian side 6 million euros. Spartak fans compared Vidic to Dolph Lundgren who played the Russian boxer, Ivan Drago, in the movie *Rocky IV*.

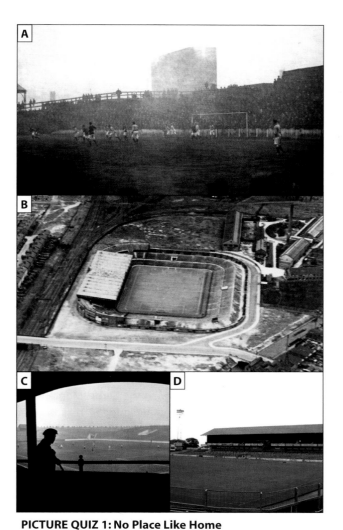

PICTURE QUIZ 1: No Place Like Home

Name these four United "home" grounds – some more temporary residences than others.

PICTURE QUIZ 2: Reader, I Married Him

Who are they? And name their respective United spouses.

PICTURE QUIZ 3: The Apprentice

These four footballers went on to be the manager at Old Trafford. Can you name them?

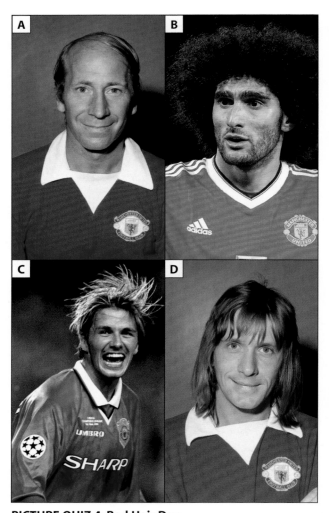

PICTURE QUIZ 4: Bad Hair Day

Who are the four follicly challenged or curiously coiffeured United men?

PICTURE QUIZ 5: Eric's Oeuvre

Name the movies in which Eric Cantona appeared.

PICTURE QUIZ 6: Mystery Men at the Euros
Who are these four United players experiencing the agonies of Euro 2016? And which countries did they represent in France?

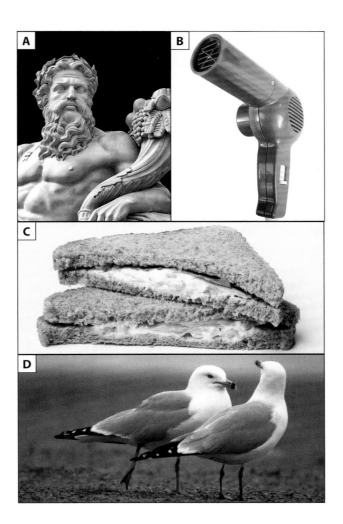

PICTURE QUIZ 7: Remind You of Anyone?
Some things get you thinking outside the box. Which
United heroes immediately spring to mind?

PICTURE QUIZ 8: Wear It With Pride

Here are some Manchester United away kits to marvel at.
Name the season and the United star doing the modelling.

ANSWERS ON PAGE 188

Red Devil turned Black Cat

Manchester United's on-loan defender, Jonny Evans was named Young Player of the Year when Sunderland held its annual Player of the Year Awards night at the Stadium of Light on 1 May 2007. A Northern Ireland international, Evans played for United in friendlies in 2006, and also in that year's Amsterdam tournament, he made his senior debut for the Reds on 26 September 2007 in the League Cup.

Happy half century

When Manchester United travelled to play Newcastle United at St James's Park on 1 January 2007, it was their 50th match played on New Year's Day. The game ended 2–2, Paul Scholes scoring both of United's goals.

Super Swede quick off the mark

Swedish legend Henrik Larsson came to Old Trafford on a three-month loan spell from his home club Helsingborg and made a scoring debut for United in a 2–1 FA Cup third round win over Aston Villa at Old Trafford on 7 January 2007. At Scottish giants Celtic, he had won just about every domestic medal and with Barcelona he won a UEFA Champions League winner's medal. Helsingborg offered to extend his loan deal at United until the end of the season, but Larsson declined it.

Kind invitation

When Wolverhampton Wanderers were crowned Champions in season 1957–58, UEFA issued United with an invitation to participate in the 1958–59 European Cup despite United finishing 9th in the League. It was a gesture of respect from European football's governing body for the sorrow felt for United by all football fans following the Munich Air Disaster. However, the Football League refused United permission to participate, perhaps exercising some form of twisted revenge for Matt Busby's defiance in leading United into Europe in season 1956–57 against their wishes. But Matt got his revenge a decade later when United were crowned Champions of Europe.

FourFourTwo awards

The football magazine, *FourFourTwo*, conducted a poll in March 1995 to find the 100 greatest footballers of all time. The judges included Sepp Blatter, Michel Platini and Gordon Taylor. No fewer than 13 Manchester United players made the Top 100 with George Best the highest placed in third position. The others were:

ERIC CANTONA	F	*BOBBY CHARLTON*
DUNCAN EDWARDS	F	*RYAN GIGGS*
MARK HUGHES	F	*ANDREI KANCHELSKIS*
DENIS LAW	F	*ARNOLD MUHREN*
JESPER OLSEN	F	*ALBERT QUIXALL*
BRYAN ROBSON	F	*GORDON STRACHAN*

The Coronation Cup

In 1953 Manchester United participated in the Coronation Cup that was held to commemorate the crowning of Queen Elizabeth II. The top teams in England and Scotland were invited, and United beat Glasgow Rangers 2–1 in the first round before losing 2–1 in the semi-final at Hampden Park to the eventual winners, Celtic.

Fortress Old Trafford

United won their final League home game of the 1982–83 season, beating Luton Town 3–0, and finished third in Division One. The win meant that United were unbeaten at Old Trafford, in all competitions, throughout the season and thereby equalled their previous achievements during seasons 1896–97 and 1955–56. In all, United played 29 games at home: 21 League, 2 FA Cup, 5 League Cup and 1 UEFA Cup.

Bad light stops play

The kick-off to the Manchester United vs. West Ham United Premier League game at Old Trafford on 10 January 1999 was delayed due to a power failure in the Trafford area of Manchester. The 45 minutes extra waiting time clearly did not affect United as they ran out 4–1 winners with two goals from Andy Cole and one each from Ole Gunnar Solskjaer and Dwight Yorke.

Billy the Whizz

William "Billy" Meredith was born in Chirk, North Wales on 30 July 1874. Billy joined United from neighbours, Manchester City, in May 1906 amidst a bribes and illegal payments scandal that resulted in Billy and several of his City team-mates receiving lengthy suspensions from the Football Association. In 1909 Billy collected an FA Cup winners medal with United and was an important member of their Championship winning sides in 1908 and 1911.

Saving their blushes

United could only manage a draw with non-League Walthamstow Avenue in their FA Cup Fourth Round game at Old Trafford on 31 January 1953. In the replay, played at Arsenal Stadium, United won 5–2.

'Cos I'm not worth it

Elijah Round played two games in goal for United, losing 3–2 at Liverpool on 9 October 1909 and suffering a 7–1 defeat at Aston Villa on 26 February 1910. In May 1912 United transfer listed the hapless Elijah for £25. Round appealed twice to have the fee removed but was unsuccessful on both attempts. Elijah was signed from Charlton Athletic by United to act as an understudy to Harry Moger. Round was a total abstainer and did not smoke.

Victims of the Munich air disaster

The eight Busby Babes who lost their lives in the Munich crash on 6 February 1958 were: Geoff Bent, Roger Byrne, Eddie Colman, Mark Jones, David Pegg, Tommy Taylor, Liam Whelan and Duncan Edwards. Three other members of the Manchester United staff also perished: Walter Crickmer, the club secretary, first-team trainer Tom Curry and coach Bert Whalley. The other victims included eight of the nine journalists on the plane (Alf Clarke, Don Davies, George Follows, Tom Jackson, Archie Ledbrooke, Henry Rose, Frank Swift and Eric Thompson), one of the aircrew, the travel agent who arranged the trip, a supporter and two other passengers. In all, 23 people died in the crash, with Edwards and Captain Rayment dying in hospital from their injuries.

Sixteen of the 39 people on board survived the crash. Two United players amongst those who survived, Jackie Blanchflower and Johnny Berry, were so badly injured that they were never able to play competitive football again. The Munich Air Disaster remains, without doubt, one of football's blackest days.

Two out of three ain't bad

In 1994 United narrowly missed out on a unique domestic Treble of League Championship, FA Cup and League Cup when they were beaten 3–1 by Aston Villa in the League Cup final. It was the first time a team had reached the final of both domestic cup competitions and won the League Championship in the same season.

Wayne's U-Turn

On 19 October 2010, Sir Alex Ferguson informed the media that Wayne Rooney wanted to leave Manchester United, having recently decided against signing an extension to his contract which expired at the end of the 2011–12 season. Three days later the United striker made a surprise U-turn on his decision and signed a new five-year contract with the club.

Berbatov's quintet

Dimitar Berbatov scored five goals in United's crushing 7–1 defeat of Blackburn Rovers at Old Trafford on 27 November 2010 in the Premier League. The win kept United on top of the Premiership table with Ji-Sung Park and Nani also on the score sheet.

Gary calls it quits

Gary Neville announced his retirement from playing on 2 February 2011. Gary played 602 games for United since making his debut for the club in September 1992. He won a total of 14 major trophies at United and was also capped 85 times for England. Not long after he took his decision to retire Gary was appointed an Ambassador for the club and secured a job with Sky Sports. When he retired he was the longest serving member of the United squad behind Ryan Giggs.

Out on his own

On 16 August 2010, Ryan Giggs maintained his record of scoring in every Premier League season since the inaugural campaign in 1992–93. Giggsy scored in United's 3–0 win over Newcastle United at Old Trafford in their opening game of the 2010–11 season. Given that Ryan also scored for United in the First Division in seasons 1990–91 and 1991–92, in total he scored in 21 successive campaigns in the top flight of English football. On 6 March 2011, Ryan Giggs surpassed Sir Bobby Charlton's League appearance record for Manchester United when he played his 607th game for United against Liverpool, eventually finishing with 672. On 14 September 2011, Giggsy scored against Benfica in the UEFA Champions League thereby becoming the oldest goal scorer in Champions League history.

Wembley dream not relived

On 28 May 2011, Manchester United faced FC Barcelona at Wembley Stadium in the UEFA Champions League Final. United were hoping to win the coveted trophy for a fourth time at the stadium where they lifted their first back in 1968. Alas, the Spanish Champions were simply just too good for the then 19-times Champions of England and lifted the European Cup/UEFA Champions League trophy for the fourth time in their history with a comfortable 3–1 victory. Interestingly the 2011 final was the 19th in the UEFA Champions League era. The 2011 final was United's third final in four years and their fifth final overall.

CHAPTER

2

WE ARE THE CHAMPIONS

In the past 25 years, nowhere in England has the classic track "We Are the Champions" by rock group Queen been played more often than at "the Theatre of Dreams", Old Trafford. Such has been Manchester United's complete dominance of the competition, since 1992–93, the inaugural season of the FA Premier League, United have finished the campaign as the champions 13 times; everyone else has finished top of the pile a combined twelve times.

But League success has not been confined to the past quarter-century United won the Football League championship – when it was Division One and the Football League comprised just 40 clubs – for the first time as far back as 1907–08. Six more Football League titles would be celebrated over the following 60 years before Sir Alex Ferguson returned United to the forefront of the English game. When you read on you will find a brief report of every one of the record-breaking 20 Football League Division One and Premier League titles, together with a League table showing United top of the pile.

There is glory that comes with winning cup finals, but the true judgement of a club's greatness comes with winning the league title – for this is the ultimate proof of quality and consistency over the course of a long and gruelling nine-month campaign.

1907–08

Manchester United's first Football League championship was achieved long before the final day of the season, a 2–1 victory over Preston North End, with goals coming from Harry Halse, and a Rodway own goal. It was a dominant performance by the club, as they finished nine points clear of the chasing pack. In winning the Championship, United set a then season record for the most League points – 52.

DID YOU KNOW THAT?
United were so far clear of the rest of the field that runners-up Aston Villa were only one point closer to the champions than they were to a relegation position.

		P	W	D	L	F	A	W	D	L	F	A	Pts
1.	**Manchester United**	38	15	1	3	43	19	8	5	6	38	29	52
2.	Aston Villa	38	9	6	4	47	24	8	3	8	30	35	43
3.	Manchester City	38	12	5	2	36	19	4	6	9	26	35	43
4.	Newcastle United	38	11	4	4	41	24	4	8	7	24	30	42
5.	Sheffield Wednesday	38	14	0	5	50	25	5	4	10	23	39	42
6.	Middlesbrough	38	12	2	5	32	16	5	9	22	29	41
7.	Bury	38	8	7	4	29	22	6	4	9	29	39	39
8.	Liverpool	38	11	2	6	43	24	5	4	10	25	37	38
9.	Nottingham Forest	38	11	6	2	42	21	2	5	12	17	41	37
10.	Bristol City	38	8	7	4	29	21	4	5	10	29	40	36
11.	Everton	38	11	4	4	34	24	4	2	13	24	40	36
12.	Preston North End	38	9	7	3	33	18	3	5	11	14	35	36
13.	Chelsea	38	8	3	8	30	35	6	5	8	23	27	36
14=	Arsenal	38	9	8	2	32	18	3	4	12	19	45	36
14=	Blackburn Rovers	38	10	7	2	35	23	2	5	12	16	40	36
16.	Sunderland	38	11	1	2	6	53	31	5	1	13	25	44	35
17.	Sheffield United	38	8	6	5	27	22	4	5	10	25	36	35
18.	Notts County	38	9	3	7	24	19	4	5	10	15	32	34
19.	Bolton Wanderers	38	10	3	6	35	26	4	2	13	17	32	33
20.	Birmingham City	38	6	6	7	22	28	3	6	10	18	32	30

1910–11

United's second Football League title in three seasons was nothing like as simple as the stroll they had previously enjoyed, although they amassed the same points total, 52. With Aston Villa right on their heels, United needed to win their final match of the season, against Sunderland at Old Trafford, to take the crown. They did it in some style, winning 5–1 with goals from Harry Halse, two, Fred Turnbull, Enoch West, and a Milton own goal. It would be United's last League championship for 41 years.

DID YOU KNOW THAT?
This was Manchester United's first full season at Old Trafford. The first game there had been on 19 February 1910.

		P	W	D	L	F	A	W	D	L	F	A	Pts
1.	**Manchester United**	38	14	4	1	47	18	8	4	7	25	22	52
2.	Aston Villa	38	15	3	1	50	18	7	4	8	19	23	51
3.	Sunderland	38	10	6	3	44	22	5	9	5	23	26	45
4.	Everton	38	12	3	4	34	17	7	4	8	16	19	45
5.	Bradford City	38	13	1	5	33	16	7	4	8	18	26	45
6.	Sheffield Wednesday	38	10	5	4	24	15	7	3	9	23	33	42
7.	Oldham Athletic	38	13	4	2	30	12	3	5	11	14	29	41
8.	Newcastle United	38	8	7	4	37	18	7	3	9	24	25	40
9.	Sheffield United	38	8	3	8	27	21	7	5	7	22	22	38
10.	Arsenal	38	9	6	4	24	14	4	6	9	17	35	38
11.	Notts County	38	9	6	4	21	16	5	4	10	16	29	38
12.	Blackburn Rovers	38	12	2	5	40	14	1	9	9	22	40	37
13.	Liverpool	38	11	3	5	38	19	4	4	11	15	34	37
14.	Preston North End	38	8	5	6	25	19	4	6	9	15	30	35
15.	Tottenham Hotspur	38	10	5	4	40	23	3	1	15	12	40	32
16.	Middlesbrough	38	9	5	5	31	21	2	5	12	18	42	32
17.	Manchester City	38	7	5	7	26	26	2	8	9	17	32	31
18.	Bury	38	8	9	2	27	18	1	2	16	16	53	29
19.	Bristol City	38	8	4	7	23	21	3	1	15	20	45	27
20.	Nottingham Forest	38	5	4	10	28	31	4	3	12	27	44	25

1951–52

It is always dramatic when a championship race comes down to the final match and so it was in May 1952, when Arsenal visited Old Trafford. United had a two-point lead (there were two points for a win in those days), so a draw would have been enough. But United dominated and ran out 6–1 winners. Jack Rowley scored a hat-trick while Stan Pearson (2) and Roger Byrne were the other goalscorers.

DID YOU KNOW THAT?
With a much better goal average, United knew that Arsenal would have needed a 7–0 win to snatch the title from them.

		P	W	D	L	F	A	W	D	L	F	A	Pts
1.	**Manchester United**	42	15	3	3	55	21	8	8	5	40	31	57
2.	Tottenham Hotspur	42	16	1	4	45	20	6	8	7	31	31	53
3.	Arsenal	42	13	7	1	54	30	8	4	9	26	31	53
4.	Portsmouth	42	13	3	5	42	25	7	5	9	26	33	48
5.	Bolton Wanderers	42	11	7	3	35	26	8	3	10	30	35	48
6.	Aston Villa	42	13	3	5	49	28	6	6	9	30	42	47
7.	Preston North End	42	10	5	6	39	22	7	7	7	35	32	46
8.	Newcastle United	42	12	4	5	62	28	6	5	10	36	45	45
9.	Blackpool	42	12	5	4	40	27	6	4	11	24	37	45
10.	Charlton Athletic	42	12	5	4	41	24	5	5	11	27	39	44
11.	Liverpool	42	6	11	4	31	25	6	8	7	26	36	43
12.	Sunderland	42	8	6	7	41	28	7	6	8	29	33	42
13.	WBA	42	8	9	4	38	29	6	4	11	36	48	41
14.	Burnley	42	9	6	6	32	19	6	4	11	24	44	40
15.	Manchester City	42	7	5	9	29	28	6	8	7	29	33	39
16.	Wolverhampton W	42	8	6	7	40	33	4	8	9	33	40	38
17.	Derby County	42	10	4	7	43	37	5	3	13	20	43	37
18.	Middlesbrough	42	12	4	5	37	25	3	2	16	27	63	36
19.	Chelsea	42	10	3	8	31	29	4	5	12	21	43	36
20.	Stoke City	42	8	6	7	34	32	4	1	16	15	56	31
21.	Huddersfield Town	42	9	3	9	32	35	1	5	15	17	47	28
22.	Fulham	42	5	7	9	38	31	3	4	14	20	46	27

1955–56

The only issue for Manchester United, on the final day of the season was whether they could match the 11-point difference between champions and runners-up. The title had been claimed two weeks earlier and Dennis Viollet's 20th League goal of the campaign gave United a 1–0 win over Portsmouth, so they emulated the winning margin set by Preston (in 1889), Sunderland (1893) and Aston Villa (1897).

DID YOU KNOW THAT?
For the first time since moving into Old Trafford, United were undefeated at home throughout the whole League season.

		P	W	D	L	F	A	W	D	L	F	A	Pts
1.	**Manchester United**	42	18	3	0	51	20	7	7	7	32	31	60
2.	Blackpool	42	13	4	4	56	27	7	5	9	30	35	49
3.	Wolverhampton W	42	15	2	4	51	27	5	7	9	38	38	49
4.	Manchester City	42	11	5	5	40	27	7	5	9	42	42	46
5.	Arsenal	42	13	4	4	38	22	5	6	10	22	39	46
6.	Birmingham City	42	12	4	5	51	26	6	5	10	24	31	45
7.	Burnley	42	11	3	7	37	20	7	5	9	27	34	44
8.	Bolton Wanderers	42	13	3	5	50	24	5	4	12	21	34	43
9.	Sunderland	42	10	8	3	44	36	7	1	13	36	59	43
10.	Luton Town	42	12	4	5	44	27	5	4	12	22	37	42
11.	Newcastle United	42	12	4	5	49	24	5	3	13	36	46	41
12.	Portsmouth	42	9	8	4	46	38	7	1	13	32	47	41
13.	WBA	42	13	3	5	37	25	5	2	14	21	45	41
14.	Charlton Athletic	42	13	2	6	47	26	4	4	13	28	55	40
15.	Everton	42	11	5	5	37	29	4	5	12	18	40	40
16.	Chelsea	42	10	4	7	32	26	4	7	10	32	51	39
17.	Cardiff City	42	11	4	6	36	32	4	5	12	19	37	39
18.	Tottenham Hotspur	42	9	4	8	37	33	6	3	12	24	38	37
19.	Preston North End	42	6	5	10	32	36	8	3	10	41	36	36
20.	Aston Villa	42	9	6	6	32	29	2	7	12	20	40	35
21.	Huddersfield Town	42	9	4	8	32	30	5	3	13	22	53	35
22.	Sheffield United	42	8	6	7	31	35	4	3	14	32	42	33

1956-57

United dominated the 1956–57 Football League season and won the title by eight points. The Reds finished with a 1–1 home draw against West Bromwich Albion, Alex Dawson scoring. It was their second successive championship and third in five seasons. United's total of 103 League goals was a club record (it was matched two seasons later), and in all competitions they hit the back of the net 143 times.

DID YOU KNOW THAT?
United would not retain the League Championship until they won the first two Premier League titles in 1993 and 1994.

		P	W	D	L	F	A	W	D	L	F	A	Pts
1.	**Manchester United**	**42**	**14**	**4**	**3**	**55**	**25**	**14**	**4**	**3**	**48**	**29**	**64**
2.	Tottenham Hotspur	42	15	4	2	70	24	7	8	6	34	32	56
3.	Preston North End	42	15	4	2	50	19	8	6	7	34	37	56
4.	Blackpool	42	14	3	4	55	26	8	6	7	38	39	53
5.	Arsenal	42	12	5	4	45	21	9	3	9	40	48	50
6.	Wolverhampton W	42	17	2	2	70	29	3	6	12	24	41	48
7.	Burnley	42	14	5	2	41	21	4	5	12	15	29	46
8.	Leeds United	42	10	8	3	42	18	5	6	10	30	45	44
9.	Bolton Wanderers	42	13	6	2	42	23	3	6	12	23	42	44
10.	Aston Villa	42	10	8	3	45	25	4	7	10	20	30	43
11.	WBA	42	8	8	5	31	25	6	6	9	28	36	42
12.	Birmingham City	42	12	5	4	52	25	3	4	14	17	44	39
13.	Chelsea	42	7	8	6	43	36	6	5	10	30	37	39
14.	Sheffield Wednesday	42	14	3	4	55	29	2	3	16	27	59	38
15.	Everton	42	10	5	6	34	28	4	5	12	27	51	38
16.	Luton Town	42	10	4	7	32	26	4	5	12	26	50	37
17.	Newcastle United	42	10	5	6	43	31	4	3	14	24	56	36
18.	Manchester City	42	10	2	9	48	42	3	7	11	30	46	35
19.	Portsmouth	42	8	6	7	37	35	2	7	12	25	57	33
20.	Sunderland	42	9	5	7	40	30	3	3	15	27	58	32
21.	Cardiff City	42	7	6	8	35	34	3	3	15	18	54	29
22.	Charlton Athletic	42	7	3	11	31	44	2	1	18	31	76	22

1964–65

Manchester United effectively clinched their sixth League title with a 3–1 home win over Arsenal on 26 April 1965, with Denis Law, twice, and George Best on target. As goal average rather than goal difference separated teams on the same number of points, United's eventual winning margin of 0.686 of a goal over Leeds United was signifcant. Thus a final game loss, 2–1 at Aston Villa, didn't cost them the title.

DID YOU KNOW THAT?
United's chances of completing the League and FA Cup double were thwarted by Leeds, 1–0, in a semi-final replay.

		P	W	D	L	F	A	W	D	L	F	A	Pts
1.	**Manchester United**	42	16	4	1	52	13	10	5	6	37	26	61
2.	Leeds United	42	16	3	2	53	23	10	6	5	30	29	61
3.	Chelsea	42	15	2	4	48	19	9	6	6	41	35	56
4.	Everton	42	9	10	2	37	22	8	5	8	32	38	49
5.	Nottingham Forest	42	10	7	4	45	33	7	6	8	26	34	47
6.	Tottenham Hotspur	42	18	3	0	65	20	1	4	16	22	51	45
7.	Liverpool	42	12	5	4	42	33	5	5	11	25	40	44
8.	Sheffield Wednesday	42	13	5	3	37	15	3	6	12	20	40	43
9.	West Ham United	42	14	2	5	48	25	5	2	14	34	46	42
10.	Blackburn Rovers	42	12	2	7	46	33	4	8	9	37	46	42
11.	Stoke City	42	11	4	6	40	27	5	6	10	27	39	42
12.	Burnley	42	9	9	3	39	26	7	1	13	31	44	42
13.	Arsenal	42	11	5	5	42	31	6	2	13	27	44	41
14.	WBA	42	10	5	6	45	25	3	8	10	25	40	39
15.	Sunderland	42	12	6	3	45	26	2	3	16	19	48	37
16.	Aston Villa	42	14	1	6	36	24	2	4	15	21	58	37
17.	Blackpool	42	9	7	5	41	28	3	4	14	26	50	35
18.	Leicester City	42	9	6	6	43	36	2	7	12	26	49	35
19.	Sheffield United	42	7	5	9	30	29	5	6	10	20	35	35
20.	Fulham	42	10	5	6	44	32	1	7	13	16	46	34
21.	Wolverhampton W	42	8	2	11	33	36	5	2	14	26	53	30
22.	Birmingham City	42	6	8	7	36	40	2	3	16	28	56	27

1966-67

Although United experienced surprise early exits in both the FA and League Cups, their League form during the 1966–67 season was outstanding. The Reds were unbeaten in their last 20 games and they won the title on the penultimate Saturday of the season by thrashing West Ham United 6–1 at Upton Park (Denis Law, two, George Best, Bobby Charlton, Pat Crerand and Bill Foulkes scoring the United goals).

DID YOU KNOW THAT?
Norwich City's 2–1 FA Cup 4th round victory at Old Trafford was the only time United suffered a home loss in 1966–67.

		P	W	D	L	F	A	W	D	L	F	A	Pts
1.	**Manchester United**	42	17	4	0	51	13	7	8	6	33	32	60
2.	Nottingham Forest	42	16	4	1	41	13	7	6	8	23	28	56
3.	Tottenham Hotspur	42	15	3	3	44	21	9	5	7	27	27	56
4.	Leeds United	42	15	4	2	41	17	7	7	7	21	25	55
5.	Liverpool	42	12	7	2	36	17	7	6	8	28	30	51
6.	Everton	42	11	4	6	39	22	8	6	7	26	24	48
7.	Arsenal	42	11	6	4	32	20	5	8	8	26	27	46
8.	Leicester City	42	12	4	5	47	28	6	4	11	31	43	44
9.	Chelsea	42	7	9	5	33	29	8	5	8	34	33	44
10.	Sheffield United	42	11	5	5	34	22	5	5	11	18	37	42
11.	Sheffield Wednesday	42	9	7	5	39	19	5	6	10	17	28	41
12.	Stoke City	42	11	5	5	40	21	6	2	13	23	37	41
13.	WBA	42	11	1	9	40	28	5	6	10	37	45	39
14.	Burnley	42	11	4	6	43	28	4	5	12	23	48	39
15.	Manchester City	42	8	9	4	27	25	4	6	11	16	27	39
16.	West Ham United	42	8	6	7	40	31	6	2	13	40	53	36
17.	Sunderland	42	12	3	6	39	26	2	5	14	19	46	36
18.	Fulham	42	8	7	6	49	34	3	5	13	22	49	34
19.	Southampton	42	10	3	8	49	41	4	3	14	25	51	34
20.	Newcastle United	42	9	5	7	24	27	3	4	14	15	54	33
21.	Aston Villa	42	7	5	9	30	33	4	2	15	24	52	29
22.	Blackpool	42	1	5	15	18	36	5	4	12	23	40	21

1992–93

United rounded off the season as the first ever FA Premier League champions by winning 2–1 against Wimbledon at Selhurst Park on 9 May 1993 (Paul Ince and Bryan Robson scoring). The win meant that the Reds matched their best ever finish to a season – seven successive wins – first achieved in 1980–81. United won the championship by ten points from their nearest challengers, Aston Villa.

DID YOU KNOW THAT?
The inaugural FA Premier League title was officially won when United weren't playing – Alex Ferguson was on a golf course.

		P	W	D	L	F	A	W	D	L	F	A	Pts
1.	**Manchester United**	42	14	5	2	39	14	10	7	4	28	17	84
2.	Aston Villa	42	13	5	3	36	16	8	6	7	21	24	74
3.	Norwich City	42	13	6	2	31	19	8	3	10	30	46	72
4.	Blackburn Rovers	42	13	4	4	38	18	7	7	7	30	28	71
5.	QPR	42	11	5	5	41	32	6	7	8	22	24	63
6.	Liverpool	42	13	4	4	41	18	3	7	11	21	37	59
7.	Sheffield Wednesday	42	9	8	4	34	26	6	6	9	21	25	59
8.	Tottenham Hotspur	42	11	5	5	40	25	5	6	10	20	41	59
9.	Manchester City	42	7	8	6	30	25	8	4	9	26	26	57
10.	Arsenal	42	8	6	7	25	20	7	5	9	15	18	56
11.	Chelsea	42	9	7	5	29	22	5	7	9	22	32	56
12.	Wimbledon	42	9	4	8	33	23	5	8	8	24	32	54
13.	Everton	42	7	6	8	26	27	8	2	11	27	28	53
14.	Sheffield United	42	10	6	5	33	19	4	4	13	21	34	52
15.	Coventry City	42	7	4	10	29	28	6	9	6	23	29	52
16.	Ipswich Town	42	8	9	4	29	22	4	7	10	21	33	52
17.	Leeds United	42	12	8	1	40	17	0	7	14	17	45	51
18.	Southampton	42	10	6	5	30	21	3	5	13	24	40	50
19.	Oldham Athletic	42	10	6	5	43	30	3	4	14	20	44	49
20.	Crystal Palace	42	6	9	6	27	25	5	7	9	21	36	49
21.	Middlesbrough	42	8	5	8	33	27	3	6	12	21	48	44
22.	Nottingham Forest	42	6	4	11	17	25	4	6	11	24	37	40

1993–94

After winning the inaugural FA Premier League in season 1992–93, United went one better the following year when they retained their crown. A crowd of 44,717 filled Old Trafford and applauded the champions in their season finale, a 0–0 draw with Coventry City. A week later, United lifted the FA Cup after a 4–0 win over Chelsea at Wembley to clinch their first ever domestic Double.

DID YOU KNOW THAT?
United's total of 92 points, from 42 games, was a record which lasted until Chelsea beat it in 2004–05 (38 games).

		P	W	D	L	F	A	W	D	L	F	A	Pts
1.	**Manchester United**	42	14	6	1	39	13	13	5	3	41	25	92
2.	Blackburn Rovers	42	14	5	2	31	11	11	4	6	32	25	84
3.	Newcastle United	42	14	4	3	51	14	9	4	8	31	27	77
4.	Arsenal	42	10	8	3	25	15	8	9	4	28	13	71
5.	Leeds United	42	13	6	2	37	18	5	10	6	28	21	70
6.	Wimbledon	42	12	5	4	35	21	6	6	9	21	32	65
7.	Sheffield Wednesday	42	10	7	4	48	24	6	9	6	28	30	64
8.	Liverpool	42	12	4	5	33	23	5	5	11	26	32	60
9.	QPR	42	8	7	6	32	29	8	5	8	30	32	60
10.	Aston Villa	42	8	5	8	23	18	7	7	7	23	32	57
11.	Coventry City	42	9	7	5	23	17	5	7	9	20	28	56
12.	Norwich City	42	4	9	8	26	29	8	8	5	39	32	53
13.	West Ham United	42	6	7	8	26	31	7	6	8	21	27	52
14.	Chelsea	42	11	5	5	31	20	2	7	12	18	33	51
15.	Tottenham Hotspur	42	4	8	9	29	33	7	4	10	25	26	45
16.	Manchester City	42	6	10	5	24	22	3	8	10	14	27	45
17.	Everton	42	8	4	9	26	30	4	4	13	16	33	44
18.	Southampton	42	9	2	10	30	31	3	5	13	19	35	43
19.	Ipswich Town	42	5	8	8	21	32	4	8	9	14	26	43
20.	Sheffield United	42	6	10	5	24	23	2	8	11	18	37	42
21.	Oldham Athletic	42	5	8	8	24	33	4	5	12	18	35	40
22.	Swindon Town	42	4	7	10	25	45	1	8	12	22	55	30

1995–96

On the last day of the season, Newcastle United had to beat Tottenham Hotspur at St James' Park and hope that Middlesbrough could beat United at the Riverside Stadium in order for the Geordies to pip the Reds for the title. But United were in championship form and beat Boro 3–0 (David May, Andrew Cole and Ryan Giggs got the goals). Newcastle, meanwhile, could only manage a 1–1 draw with Spurs so United, after waiting 26 years for a title, claimed their third in four seasons.

DID YOU KNOW THAT?
United became the first English team to do the Double twice when they beat Liverpool 1–0 in the FA Cup final.

		P	W	D	L	F	A	W	D	L	F	A	Pts
1	**Manchester United**	38	15	4	0	36	9	10	3	6	37	26	82
2	Newcastle United	38	17	1	1	38	9	7	5	7	28	28	78
3	Liverpool	38	14	4	1	46	13	6	7	6	24	21	71
4	Aston Villa	38	11	5	3	32	15	7	4	8	20	20	63
5	Arsenal	38	10	7	2	30	16	7	5	7	19	16	63
6	Everton	38	10	5	4	35	19	7	5	7	29	25	61
7	Blackburn Rovers	38	14	2	3	44	19	4	5	10	17	28	61
8	Tottenham Hotspur	38	9	5	5	26	19	7	8	4	24	19	61
9	Nottingham Forest	38	11	6	2	29	17	4	7	8	21	37	58
10	West Ham United	38	9	5	5	25	21	5	4	10	18	31	51
11	Chelsea	38	7	7	5	30	22	5	7	7	16	22	50
12	Middlesbrough	38	8	3	8	27	27	3	7	9	8	23	43
13	Leeds United	38	8	3	8	21	21	4	4	11	19	36	43
14	Wimbledon	38	5	6	8	27	33	5	5	9	28	37	41
15	Sheffield Wednesday	38	7	5	7	30	31	3	5	11	18	30	40
16	Coventry City	38	6	7	6	21	23	2	7	10	21	37	38
17	Southampton	38	7	7	5	21	18	2	4	13	13	34	38
18	Manchester City	38	7	7	5	21	19	2	4	13	12	39	38
19	Queens Park Rangers	38	6	5	8	25	26	3	1	15	13	31	33
20	Bolton Wanderers	38	5	4	10	16	31	3	1	15	23	40	29

1996–97

United won their fourth FA Premier League title in five years, ending their season with a 2–0 home win over West Ham United (Ole Gunnar Solskjaer and Jordi Cruyff scoring). After the game, a unique event was witnessed by the 55,249-strong crowd and those watching on television. United's four teams paraded the four league trophies they had won: the FA Carling Premiership, Pontins League Premier Division, Lancashire League Division One and Lancashire League Division Two. It was the club's first ever clean sweep of championships.

DID YOU KNOW THAT?

Eric Cantona, United's talisman, announced his retirement from football soon after the end of the season.

		P	W	D	L	F	A	W	D	L	F	A	Pts
1.	**Manchester United**	38	12	5	2	38	17	9	7	3	38	27	75
2.	Newcastle United	38	13	3	3	54	20	6	8	5	19	20	68
3.	Arsenal	38	10	5	4	36	18	9	6	4	26	14	68
4.	Liverpool	38	10	6	3	38	19	9	5	5	24	18	68
5.	Aston Villa	38	11	5	3	27	13	6	5	8	20	21	61
6.	Chelsea	38	9	8	2	33	22	7	3	9	25	33	59
7.	Sheffield Wednesday	38	8	10	1	25	16	6	5	8	25	35	57
8.	Wimbledon	38	9	6	4	28	21	6	5	8	21	25	56
9.	Leicester City	38	7	5	7	22	26	5	6	8	24	28	47
10.	Tottenham Hotspur	38	8	4	7	19	17	5	3	11	25	34	46
11.	Leeds United	38	7	7	5	15	13	4	6	9	13	25	46
12.	Derby County	38	8	6	5	25	22	3	7	9	20	36	46
13.	Blackburn Rovers	38	8	4	7	28	23	1	11	7	14	20	42
14.	West Ham United	38	7	6	6	27	25	3	6	10	12	23	42
15.	Everton	38	7	4	8	24	22	3	8	8	20	35	42
16.	Southampton	38	6	7	6	32	24	4	4	11	18	32	41
17.	Coventry City	38	4	8	7	19	23	5	6	8	19	31	41
18.	Sunderland	38	7	6	6	20	18	3	4	12	15	35	40
19.	Middlesbrough*	38	8	5	6	34	25	2	7	10	17	35	39
20.	Nottingham Forest	38	3	9	7	15	27	3	7	9	16	32	34

Middlesbrough deducted 3 points for failing to fulfil fixture.

1998–99

After going head-to-head with Arsenal all season, the Championship came down to the final day. United had to beat Spurs to regain their trophy from their London rivals. A crowd of 55,189 packed Old Trafford and was stunned into silence when Les Ferdinand put the visitors in front. Arsenal fans put their dislike of their North London rivals to one side for the day and were ecstatic when United fell behind. However, a David Beckham drive from the edge of the area put United level at the interval and in the second half, Andy Cole, who came on as a substitute for Teddy Sheringham, lobbed a delicate chip over Ian Walker to give United championship glory. United had claimed the first leg of the illustrious Treble, their fifth Premiership crown.

		P	W	D	L	F	A	W	D	L	F	A	Pts
1.	**Manchester United**	38	14	4	1	45	18	8	9	2	35	19	79
2.	Arsenal	38	14	5	0	34	5	8	7	4	25	12	78
3.	Chelsea	38	12	6	1	29	13	8	9	2	28	17	75
4.	Leeds United	38	12	5	2	32	9	6	8	5	30	25	67
5.	West Ham United	38	11	3	5	32	26	5	6	8	14	27	57
6.	Aston Villa	38	10	3	6	33	28	5	7	7	18	18	55
7.	Liverpool	38	10	5	4	44	24	5	4	10	24	25	54
8.	Derby County	38	8	7	4	22	19	5	6	8	18	26	52
9.	Middlesbrough	38	7	9	3	25	18	5	6	8	23	36	51
10.	Leicester City	38	7	6	6	25	25	5	7	7	15	21	49
11.	Tottenham Hotspur	38	7	7	5	28	26	4	7	8	19	24	47
12.	Sheffield Wednesday	38	7	5	7	20	15	6	2	11	21	27	46
13.	Newcastle United	38	7	6	6	26	25	4	7	8	22	29	46
14.	Everton	38	6	8	5	22	12	5	2	12	20	35	43
15.	Coventry City	38	8	6	5	26	21	3	3	13	13	30	42
16.	Wimbledon	38	7	7	5	22	21	3	5	11	18	42	42
17.	Southampton	38	9	4	6	29	26	2	4	13	8	38	41
18.	Charlton Athletic	38	4	7	8	20	20	4	5	10	21	36	36
19.	Blackburn Rovers	38	6	5	8	21	24	1	9	9	17	28	35
20.	Nottingham Forest	38	3	7	9	18	31	4	2	13	17	38	30

1999-2000

United lifted their sixth Premier League Championship in only eight seasons with an exhilarating end-of-season title-winning run. After stuttering in February, United drew 1–1 at home to Liverpool on 4 March 2000. But the Reds won all of their last 11 League games, including a 7–1 home rout of West Ham United (Paul Scholes, three, Andrew Cole, Dennis Irwin, David Beckham and Ole-Gunnar Solskjaer scoring), and a season-ending 1–0 win at Aston Villa (Teddy Sheringham).

DID YOU KNOW THAT?

As UEFA Champions League winners in 1999, United were invited to play in the inaugural FIFA World Club Cup in Brazil, so the FA Cup-holding Reds pulled out of the 1999–2000 edition.

		P	W	D	L	F	A	W	D	L	F	A	Pts
1.	**Manchester United**	38	15	4	0	59	16	13	3	3	38	29	91
2.	Arsenal	38	14	3	2	42	17	8	4	7	31	26	73
3.	Leeds United	38	12	2	5	29	18	9	4	6	29	25	69
4.	Liverpool	38	11	4	4	28	13	8	6	5	23	17	67
5.	Chelsea	38	12	5	2	35	12	6	6	7	18	22	65
6.	Aston Villa	38	8	8	3	23	12	7	5	7	23	23	58
7.	Sunderland	38	10	6	3	28	17	6	4	9	29	39	58
8.	Leicester City	38	10	3	6	31	24	6	4	9	24	31	55
9.	West Ham United	38	11	5	3	32	23	4	5	10	20	30	55
10.	Tottenham Hotspur	38	10	3	6	40	26	5	5	9	17	23	53
11.	Newcastle United	38	10	5	4	42	20	4	5	10	21	34	52
12.	Middlesbrough	38	8	5	6	23	26	6	5	8	23	26	52
13.	Everton	38	7	9	3	36	21	5	5	9	23	28	50
14.	Coventry City	38	12	1	6	38	22	0	7	12	9	32	44
15.	Southampton	38	8	4	7	26	22	4	4	11	19	40	44
16.	Derby County	38	6	3	10	22	25	3	8	8	22	32	38
17.	Bradford City	38	6	8	5	26	29	3	1	15	12	39	36
18.	Wimbledon	38	6	7	6	30	28	1	5	13	16	46	33
19.	Sheffield Wednesday	38	6	3	10	21	23	2	4	13	17	47	31
20.	Watford	38	5	4	10	24	31	1	2	16	11	46	24

2000–01

The highlight of a second straight dominant season for United came on 25 February 2001, when their nearest rivals, Arsenal came to Old Trafford. A Gunners win might have put doubt in United minds, but Dwight Yorke grabbed a first-half hat-trick and there were goals for Roy Keane, Ole Gunnar Solskjaer and Teddy Sheringham in a 6–1 rout that showed Arsenal to be pretenders rather than contenders for the Reds' crown. United's season ended on a disappointing note, a 3–1 loss at Tottenham Hotspur, but the title was still won by 10 points.

DID YOU KNOW THAT?
Sir Alex Ferguson became the first manager to be in charge of a team winning the League title in three consecutive seasons

		P	W	D	L	F	A	W	D	L	F	A	Pts
1.	**Manchester United**	38	15	2	2	49	12	9	6	4	30	19	80
2.	Arsenal	38	15	3	1	45	13	5	7	7	18	25	70
3.	Liverpool	38	13	4	2	40	14	7	5	7	31	25	69
4.	Leeds United	38	11	3	5	36	21	9	5	5	28	22	68
5.	Ipswich Town	38	11	5	3	31	15	9	1	9	26	27	66
6.	Chelsea	38	13	3	3	44	20	4	7	8	24	25	61
7.	Sunderland	38	9	7	3	24	16	6	5	8	22	25	57
8.	Aston Villa	38	8	8	3	27	20	5	7	7	19	23	54
9.	Charlton Athletic	38	11	5	3	31	19	3	5	11	19	38	52
10.	Southampton	38	11	2	6	27	22	3	8	8	13	26	52
11.	Newcastle United	38	10	4	5	26	17	4	5	10	18	33	51
12.	Tottenham Hotspur	38	11	6	2	31	16	2	4	13	16	38	49
13.	Leicester City	38	10	4	5	28	23	4	2	13	11	28	48
14.	Middlesbrough	38	4	7	8	18	23	5	8	6	26	21	42
15.	West Ham United	38	6	6	7	24	20	4	6	9	21	30	42
16.	Everton	38	6	8	5	29	27	5	1	13	16	32	42
17.	Derby County	38	8	7	4	23	24	2	5	12	14	35	42
18.	Manchester City	38	4	3	12	20	31	4	7	8	21	34	34
19.	Coventry City	38	4	7	8	14	23	4	3	12	22	40	34
20.	Bradford City	38	4	7	8	20	29	1	4	14	10	41	26

2002–03

"We Got Our Trophy Back" was the song being sung by United fans as David Beckham and Ruud van Nistelrooy goals brought a 2–1 win at Everton on the final day of the season. In what was a long and hard campaign, United rose to the top at the end to claim their eighth Premiership crown in 11 seasons after a titanic battle with Arsenal. However, United's home form was exceptional, with 16 wins, two draws and one loss (0–1 to Bolton Wanderers) in 19 League games, scoring 42 goals and conceding only 12.

DID YOU KNOW THAT?

United lost five times in their first 19 games, but a 3–1 Boxing Day defeat at Middlesbrough was their last of the season.

		P	W	D	L	F	A	W	D	L	F	A	Pts
1.	**Manchester United**	**38**	**16**	**2**	**1**	**42**	**12**	**9**	**6**	**4**	**32**	**22**	**83**
2.	Arsenal	38	15	2	2	47	20	8	7	4	38	22	78
3.	Newcastle United	38	15	2	2	36	17	6	4	9	27	31	69
4.	Chelsea	38	12	5	2	41	15	7	5	7	27	23	67
5.	Liverpool	38	9	8	2	30	16	9	2	8	31	25	64
6.	Blackburn Rovers	38	9	7	3	24	15	7	5	7	28	28	60
7.	Everton	38	11	5	3	28	19	6	3	10	20	30	59
8.	Southampton	38	9	8	2	25	16	4	5	10	18	30	52
9.	Manchester City	38	9	2	8	28	26	6	4	9	19	28	51
10.	Tottenham Hotspur	38	9	4	6	30	29	5	4	10	21	33	50
11.	Middlesbrough	38	10	7	2	36	21	3	3	13	12	23	49
12.	Charlton Athletic	38	8	3	8	26	30	6	4	9	19	26	49
13.	Birmingham City	38	8	5	6	25	23	5	4	10	16	26	48
14.	Fulham	38	11	3	5	26	18	2	6	11	15	32	48
15.	Leeds United	38	7	3	9	25	26	7	2	10	33	31	47
16.	Aston Villa	38	11	1	6	25	14	1	7	11	17	33	45
17.	Bolton Wanderers	38	7	8	4	27	24	3	6	10	14	27	44
18.	West Ham United	38	5	7	7	21	24	5	5	9	21	35	42
19.	WBA	38	3	5	11	17	34	3	3	13	12	31	26
20.	Sunderland	38	3	2	14	11	31	1	5	13	10	34	19

2006–07

After a three-year gap, United returned to the top of the FA Premier League pile, claiming the championship by six points from Chelsea, with Liverpool and Arsenal a further 15 points behind. Even though the Reds suffered a shock 1–0 defeat at home to West Ham United on the final day of the season, they had done more than enough to clinch Premier League championship number nine, winning 28 out of 38 matches, four more than Chelsea, who were held to 11 draws during the season.

DID YOU KNOW THAT?
Dreams of another Treble were dashed by Milan in the UEFA Champions League semi-final and Chelsea in the FA Cup final.

		P	W	D	L	F	A	W	D	L	F	A	Pts
1.	**Manchester United**	38	15	2	2	46	12	13	3	3	37	15	89
2.	Chelsea	38	12	7	0	37	11	12	4	3	27	13	83
3.	Liverpool	38	14	4	1	39	7	6	4	9	18	20	68
4.	Arsenal	38	12	6	1	43	16	7	5	7	20	19	68
5.	Tottenham Hotspur	38	12	3	4	34	22	5	6	8	23	32	60
6.	Everton	38	11	4	4	33	17	4	9	6	19	19	58
7.	Bolton Wanderers	38	9	5	5	26	20	7	3	9	21	32	56
8.	Reading	38	11	2	6	29	20	5	5	9	23	27	55
9.	Portsmouth	38	11	5	3	28	15	3	7	9	17	27	54
10.	Blackburn Rovers	38	9	3	7	31	25	6	4	9	21	29	52
11.	Aston Villa	38	7	8	4	20	14	4	9	6	23	27	50
12.	Middlesbrough	38	10	3	6	31	24	2	7	10	13	25	46
13.	Newcastle United	38	7	7	5	23	20	4	3	12	15	27	43
14.	Manchester City	38	5	6	8	10	16	6	3	10	19	28	42
15.	West Ham United	38	8	2	9	24	26	4	3	12	11	33	41
16.	Fulham	38	7	7	5	18	18	1	8	10	20	42	39
17.	Wigan Athletic	38	5	4	10	18	30	5	4	10	19	29	38
18.	Sheffield United	38	7	6	6	24	21	3	2	14	8	34	38
19.	Charlton Athletic	38	7	5	7	19	20	1	5	13	15	40	34
20.	Watford	38	3	9	7	19	25	2	4	13	10	34	28

2007–08

The 2007–08 Premier League championship went to United thanks to the division's most potent attack and stingiest defence. They scored 80 goals and conceded only 22 in 38 games. United's home record, which saw them drop just four points was also a factor as they finished two clear of Chelsea and four ahead of Arsenal. On the final day, Manchester United won 2–0 at Wigan Athletic, Cristiano Ronaldo and Ryan Giggs scoring, while Chelsea drew at home to Bolton Wanderers, so more than goal difference decided the title.

DID YOU KNOW THAT?
United and Chelsea battled it out in Europe, too, until the Reds won the UEFA Champions League final penalty shoot-out.

		P	W	D	L	F	A	W	D	L	F	A	Pts
1.	**Manchester United**	38	17	1	1	47	7	10	5	4	33	15	87
2.	Chelsea	38	12	7	0	36	13	13	3	3	29	13	85
3.	Arsenal	38	14	5	0	37	11	10	6	3	37	20	83
4.	Liverpool	38	12	6	1	43	13	9	7	3	24	15	76
5.	Everton	38	11	4	4	34	17	8	4	7	21	16	65
6.	Aston Villa	38	10	3	6	34	22	6	9	4	37	29	60
7.	Blackburn Rovers	38	8	7	4	26	19	7	6	6	24	29	58
8.	Posrtsmouth	38	7	8	4	24	14	9	1	9	24	26	57
9.	Manchester City	38	11	4	4	28	20	4	6	9	17	33	55
10.	West Ham United	38	7	7	5	24	24	6	3	10	18	26	49
11.	Tottenham Hotspur	38	8	5	6	46	34	3	8	8	20	27	46
12.	Newcastle United	38	8	5	6	25	26	3	5	11	20	39	43
13.	Middlesbrough	38	7	5	7	27	23	3	7	9	16	30	42
14.	Wigan Athletic	38	8	5	6	21	17	2	5	12	13	34	40
15.	Sunderland	38	9	3	7	23	21	2	3	14	13	38	39
16.	Bolton	38	7	5	7	23	18	2	5	12	13	36	37
17.	Fulham	38	5	5	9	22	31	3	7	9	16	29	36
18.	Reading	38	8	2	9	19	25	2	4	13	22	41	36
19.	Birmingham City	38	6	8	5	30	23	2	3	14	16	39	35
20.	Derby County	38	1	5	13	12	43	0	3	16	8	46	11

2008–09

United became the first English club to win the League championship three years in a row on two occasions as they held off a determined challenge from Liverpool, with Chelsea in third place, the Blues' worst finish since 2003. After losing 4–1 to Liverpool at Old Trafford in March, United coud have wobbled, but they put together a 10-match unbeaten run, culminating in a 1–0 victory over Hull City at the KC Stadium on the last day of the season, Darron Gibson getting the all-important goal.

DID YOU KNOW THAT?
By winning their 18th League championship in 2009, United equalled the English record held by Liverpool.

		P	W	D	L	F	A	W	D	L	F	A	Pts
1	**Manchester United**	38	16	2	1	43	13	12	4	3	25	11	90
2	Liverpool	38	12	7	0	41	13	13	4	2	36	14	86
3	Chelsea	38	11	6	2	33	12	14	2	3	35	12	83
4	Arsenal	38	11	5	3	31	16	9	7	3	37	21	72
5	Everton	38	8	6	5	31	20	9	6	4	24	17	63
6	Aston Villa	38	7	9	3	27	21	10	2	7	27	27	62
7	Fulham	38	11	3	5	28	16	3	8	8	11	18	53
8	Tottenham Hotspur	38	10	5	4	21	10	4	4	11	24	35	51
9	West Ham United	38	9	2	8	23	22	5	7	7	19	23	51
10	Manchester City	38	13	0	6	40	18	2	5	12	18	32	50
11	Wigan Athletic	38	8	5	6	17	18	4	4	11	17	27	45
12	Stoke City	38	10	5	4	22	15	2	4	13	16	40	45
13	Bolton Wanderers	38	7	5	7	21	21	4	3	12	20	32	41
14	Portsmouth	38	8	3	8	26	29	2	8	9	12	28	41
15	Blackburn Rovers	38	6	7	6	22	23	4	4	11	18	37	41
16	Sunderland	38	6	3	10	21	25	3	6	10	13	29	36
17	Hull City	38	3	5	11	18	36	5	6	8	21	28	35
18	Newcastle United	38	5	7	7	24	29	2	6	11	16	30	34
19	Middlesbrough	38	5	9	5	17	20	2	2	15	11	37	32
20	West Bromwich Albion	38	7	3	9	26	33	1	5	13	10	34	32

2010-11

The 2010-11 season was United's 19th in the Premier League and ironically by winning the Premiership they claimed their 19th title to move one ahead of their bitterest of rivals, Liverpool. The season began well for United with a 3-1 win over Chelsea in the Community Shield, but it was the Londoners who set the early pace in the Premiership winning seven of their opening nine games, scoring 25 goals and conceding just two. However, just as United had done so many times in the past they got into a rhythm and were unbeaten in the Premiership until a shock 1-0 defeat away to Wolverhampton Wanderers on 5 February 2011. United went top of the table after hammering Blackburn Rovers 7-1 at Old Trafford on 27 November 2010 and remained top all the way to the finish line.

		P	W	D	L	F	A	W	D	L	F	A	Pts
1.	**Manchester United**	38	18	1	0	49	12	5	10	4	29	25	80
2.	Chelsea	38	14	3	2	39	13	7	5	7	30	20	71
3.	Manchester City	38	13	4	2	34	12	8	4	7	26	21	71
4.	Arsenal	38	11	4	4	33	15	8	7	4	39	28	68
5.	Tottenham Hotspur	38	9	9	1	30	19	7	5	7	25	27	62
6.	Liverpool	38	12	4	3	37	14	5	3	11	22	30	58
7.	Everton	38	9	7	3	31	23	4	8	7	20	22	54
8.	Fulham	38	8	7	4	30	23	3	9	7	19	20	49
9.	Aston Villa	38	8	7	4	26	19	4	5	10	22	40	48
10.	Sunderland	38	7	5	7	25	27	5	6	8	20	29	47
11.	West Bromwich Albion	38	8	6	5	30	30	4	5	10	26	41	47
12.	Newcastle United	38	6	8	5	41	27	5	5	9	15	30	46
13.	Stoke City	38	10	4	5	31	18	3	3	13	15	30	46
14.	Bolton	38	10	5	4	34	24	2	5	12	18	32	46
15.	Blackburn	38	7	7	5	22	16	4	3	12	24	43	43
16.	Wigan Athletic	38	5	8	6	22	34	4	7	8	18	27	42
17.	Wolverhampton W	38	8	4	7	30	30	3	3	13	16	36	40
18.	Birmingham City	38	6	8	5	19	22	2	7	10	18	36	39
19.	Blackpool	38	5	5	9	30	37	5	4	10	25	41	39
20.	West Ham Utd	38	5	5	9	24	31	2	7	10	19	39	33

2012–13

The 2012–13 season was Sir Alex Ferguson's last season in charge of Manchester United. On 22 April 2013, Manchester United won their 13th Premier League title and 20th English title overall following a 3-0 win at Old Trafford versus Aston Villa. It was the first time the Premier League title had been decided in April since Jose Mourinho's Chelsea lifted the trophy in 2005–06. It was Sir Alex Ferguson's 13th Premiership crown in 21 seasons with the year, 2013, particularly significant – 20 League Championships, 13 Premier League crowns.

		P	W	D	L	F	A	W	D	L	F	A	Pts
1	**Manchester United**	38	16	0	3	45	19	12	5	2	41	24	89
2	Manchester City	38	14	3	2	41	15	9	6	4	25	19	78
3	Chelsea	38	12	5	2	41	16	10	4	5	34	23	75
4	Arsenal	38	11	5	3	47	23	10	5	4	25	14	73
5	Tottenham Hotspur	38	11	5	3	29	18	10	4	5	37	28	72
6	Everton	38	12	6	1	33	17	4	9	6	22	23	63
7	Liverpool	38	9	6	4	33	16	7	7	5	38	27	61
8	West Bromwich Albion	38	9	4	6	32	25	5	3	11	21	32	49
9	Swansea City	38	6	8	5	28	26	5	5	9	19	25	46
10	West Ham United	38	9	6	4	34	22	3	4	12	11	31	46
11	Norwich City	38	8	7	4	25	20	2	7	10	16	38	44
12	Fulham	38	7	3	9	28	30	4	7	8	22	30	43
13	Stoke City	38	7	7	5	21	22	2	8	9	13	23	42
14	Southampton	38	6	7	6	26	24	3	7	9	23	36	41
15	Aston Villa	38	5	5	9	23	28	5	6	8	24	41	41
16	Newcastle United	38	9	1	9	24	31	2	7	10	21	37	41
17	Sunderland	38	5	8	6	20	19	4	4	11	21	35	39
18	Wigan Athletic	38	4	6	9	26	39	5	3	11	21	34	36
19	Reading	38	4	8	7	23	33	2	2	15	20	40	28
20	Queens Park Rangers	38	2	8	9	13	28	2	5	12	17	32	25

CHAPTER

3

MANCHESTER UNITED LEGENDS

Manchester United has been blessed to have been the home for some the finest players and managers ever seen in English, British and, indeed, world football.

On the following pages you will learn about 12 players and two managers, all of whom would rank among the greatest not only of their time, but of any era. The two managers, Sir Matt Busby and Sir Alex Ferguson are two of only a tiny handful of bosses to have received knighthoods whilst still working and all bar one of the 12 players played for one or other of them.

It is not a stretch of imagination to say that this chapter could have been extended to take up the whole book and even then, not every United legend would be featured. Players such as Billy Meredith from the early 1900s, Busby Babes Roger Byrne and Tommy Taylor, Paddy Crerand and Bill Foulkes from the 1960s, Lou Macari and Martin Buchan from the 1970s and Premier League era superstars, David Beckham, Peter Schmeichel, Gary Neville and Ruud van Nistelrooy, could all have been included without significantly diminishing the legends who appear here.

It is a testament to the greatness of Manchester United that if you were to ask 100 United fans to give their list of a baker's dozen of the Reds' greatest names, you would probably get 100 different responses.

George Best

"I have found you a genius", were the immortal words of Manchester United's Irish scout, Bill Bishop, to Matt Busby when he first saw George Best play. The young Irishman was a mesmerizing dribbler of the ball who when he was in the mood would beat a defender then do a U-turn just to show the same defender he could do it again. No wonder his team-mate, Pat Crerand, said George had "twisted blood".

Blessed with pace, precision accuracy, immaculate ball control, the ability to see a gap in a defence and exploit it, flair, charisma both on and off the pitch and a vicious body swerve that resembled a Rivelino free-kick, it was Pele who said that George Best was the greatest player in the world.

But football's first superstar, dubbed the Fifth Beatle, had a rollercoaster of a career. He made his Manchester United debut aged just 17 and whereas many of the game's true greats begin to mature and reach their peak as professional footballers in their mid-20s, George packed it all in by the age of just 26. George once famously said: "I spent a lot of money on booze, birds and fast cars. The rest I just squandered."

Two League Championships medals with United in 1965 and 1967, a European Cup winner's medal in 1968, the same year he was voted European Footballer of the Year and five-times United's top goalscorer, George had the world at his feet. But after playing is last game for United on New Year's Day 1974 George turned his back on football.

In his last 30 years George reached some lows: constant battles against alcohol, marriage splits, a liver transplant and a 12-week jail sentence in 1984 for drink-driving and assault. But it is the good times for which that George will be most remembered. His magical performance in 1966 against

Benfica in their own backyard when George scored twice in United's 5-1 win, a performance that earned him the nickname El Beatle. Or his six goals for United in the FA Cup against Northampton Town, and who will ever forget that night at Wembley on 29 May 1968 when George helped United erase the memory of the Munich Air Disaster some ten years earlier by scoring in the European Cup final in their 4-1 win over Benfica of Portugal.

George fought liver disease late in his life and underwent a transplant. Sadly, the battle was lost on 25 November 2005. His funeral attracted more than 100,000 mourners, bringing his native city to a standstill; it was likened to a state funeral.

The shy Belfast boy will forever have a special place in the hearts of every Manchester United fan.

DID YOU KNOW THAT?

George made his international debut in the same game that Pat Jennings made his. However, whereas Pat went on to win a record 119 caps for his country, George won only 37. Interestingly, George's mother was an international hockey player for Northern Ireland.

For the Record
Born: 22 May 1946, Belfast, Northern Ireland
Died: 25 November 2005, London
Country: Northern Ireland, 37 apps, 9 goals
Manchester United appearances: 470
Manchester United goals: 119
Manchester United debut: H v West Bromwich Albion, 14 September 1963, League

Sir Matt Busby, KBE, CBE

On 15 February 1945 Matt Busby was appointed manager of Manchester United and the legend began. Matt Busby was born in Bellshill, Lanarkshire in 1909. His father was a miner, who died on the Somme in World War I, and the young Busby followed in his father's footsteps down the pit. In his youth Busby always had a dream that one day he would earn his living as a footballer and in 1928 that dream became a reality when he joined Manchester City. An outstanding right-half for United's neighbours, he won an FA Cup winner's medal with them in 1934 and then moved on to Liverpool in 1936.

Matt Busby built three great teams at United. His first great side were First Division runners-up in 1947, 1948 and 1949 and winners of the FA Cup in 1948. Busby's style of management was a breath of fresh air and unlike his predecessors he joined his players on the training field, a concept unheard of at the time. Matt Busby built a dynasty at Old Trafford and put all his faith and trust in youth. The Busby Babes side of the 1950s dominated the domestic game.

During the 1950s United won the League Championship three times (1952, 1956 and 1957), were runners-up twice (1951 and 1959), FA Cup finalists in 1957 and 1958, FA Charity Shield Winners three times (1952, 1956 and 1957) and United's youth team won the first five FA Youth Cups (1953–1957).

The football world was at their feet with players such as Duncan Edwards, Eddie Colman and Bobby Charlton, all products of Matt's youth policy. However, on 6 February 1958, the heart was ripped out of Manchester United when the Elizabethan jet, carrying the players home from their

European Cup quarter-final tie with Red Star Belgrade, crashed on take-off at Munich Airport. Eight of the team died and Matt was severely injured.

The rebuilt team of the 1960s thrilled fans up and down the country with their swashbuckling style. His philosophy to his players was simply for them to go on to the field and enjoy themselves. In the 1960s United won the FA Cup in 1963, were First Division Champions in 1965 and 1967, First Division runners-up in 1964 and 1968, joint-holders of the FA Charity Shield in 1965 and 1967 and winners of the FA Youth Cup for the sixth time under his leadership in 1964. But the greatest night in Matt Busby's football life came at Wembley in May 1968 when his third great side beat Benfica of Portugal 4–1 after extra time to claim the European Cup.

Later that year he was knighted. Matt Busby was a man of the people, honest and hard working, respected by everyone and loved by the fans of his beloved Manchester United. He was, and always will be remembered as "The Father of Manchester United".

DID YOU KNOW THAT?

In 1993, the road which runs past the front of Old Trafford was renamed Sir Matt Busby Way in his honour.

For the Record

Born: 26 May 1909, Bellshill, Lanarkshire, Scotland
Died: 20 January 1994, Cheadle, Cheshire
Manchester United career: 1945–71
League Titles: 1952, 1956, 1957, 1965, 1967
FA Cup: 1948, 1963
European Cup: 1968

Eric Cantona

When Eric Cantona was sensationally transferred from Leeds United to Manchester United in November 1992, some Manchester United fans interviewed on TV questioned the signing, even going as far as to say that they would never sing, "Ooh Aah Cantona". Over the following five seasons, United won four Premier League titles, two FA Cups and two Doubles. Eric almost single-handedly re-wrote the history books of Manchester United. And as for the songs about Eric, well the United faithful are still chanting Eric's name today at Old Trafford even though he left the club in 1997!

Prior to arriving in England, Eric had led something of a nomadic footballing life, having played for Auxerre, FC Martiques, Olympique Marseille, Bordeaux, Montpellier and Nimes in his native France. Sheffield Wednesday passed up on the opportunity of signing Eric when he was on trial with them in 1991.

Sheffield Wednesday's loss was Leeds United's gain as Eric, along with former United great, Gordon Strachan, revitalised the club. They won the last First Division title (when it was also the League Championship) in 1992, with Manchester United in the runners-up position. However, it was a phone call from Howard Wilkinson to Alex Ferguson that resulted in Eric's move to Old Trafford. Wilkinson was inquiring about the availability of Denis Irwin, to which Alex replied the Irishman was not for sale but cheekily asked Wilkinson about Cantona's availability. Within days, Eric had signed for United in a £1 million transfer.

On 6 December 1992, Eric made his United debut as a substitute against Manchester City in a 2–1 home win. Eric's arrival transformed United's fortunes on the pitch with his aura of invincibility, presence, Gallic flair, grace, skill, vision, creativity, goals and, not forgetting, turned-up collar. On a number of occasions, Eric's fiery temper got him into trouble both on and off the pitch. In December 1991, Eric had appeared before a French Disciplinary Committee and was suspended for calling its members idiots. In January 1995, Eric exacted his own revenge on a Crystal Palace supporter who verbally abused him as he was walking off the pitch following a red card.

However, despite his brushes with authority, Eric will always be remembered for his genius on the pitch in the colours of Manchester United. In the games Eric played for United, they won 66 per cent, drew 23 per cent and lost only 11 per cent. The Frenchman has since translated his passion for football into a love of the arts. He once said of Manchester United: "I am in love with Manchester United. It is like finding a wife who has given me the perfect marriage."

DID YOU KNOW THAT?
In his entire Manchester United career, Eric Cantona came off the bench as a substitute only once – his debut – in the December 1992 Manchester derby at Old Trafford.

For the Record
Born: 24 May 1966, Marseille, France
Country: France, 45 apps, 20 goals
Manchester United appearances: 191
Manchester United goals: 88
Manchester United debut: H v Manchester City,
   6 December 1992, League

Sir Bobby Charlton, KBE, OBE, CBE

Bobby Charlton was born on 11 October 1937 in Ashington, a mining village in the north-east of England. His genes dictated that he would be a footballer as his mother, Cissie, was the cousin of Jackie Milburn, the legendary Newcastle United and England centre-forward and his brother Jack enjoyed a long and successful career. Added to this, his grandfather Tanner Milburn and four other uncles were all professional footballers: George, Jack and Jim Milburn all played for Leeds United, Stan Milburn for Leicester City.

On 9 February 1953 Manchester United scout, Joe Armstrong, watched 15-year-old Bobby Charlton play and speaking of the game, Joe said: "I had to peer through a mist, but what I saw was enough. This boy is going to be a world-beater." With such a precocious talent, it was no surprise that around 20 teams wanted to sign him, but Bobby had committed his future to Matt Busby's Manchester United. He became part of the famous Busby Babes, playing in three FA Youth Cup winning sides, in 1954, 1955 and 1956. On 6 October 1956 Bobby made his United debut against Charlton Athletic in a First Division match at Old Trafford, scoring twice in a 4–2 victory.

Bobby won almost everything there was to win in the game at club level; a European Cup winner's medal, three League Championship winner's medals and an FA Cup winner's medal, and he was voted European Player of the Year in 1966. On top of all that Bobby played 106 times for England, scoring a national record 49 goals, and he won the World Cup in 1966. He was the first England player to appear in four World Cup finals (1958, 1962, 1966 and 1970). The great Sir Matt Busby said of him: "He has broken all records and won everything possible that there is to win. Yet he has remained completely unspoiled."

Whereas George Best possessed the style and Denis Law was flamboyant, Bobby Charlton was a football machine. He possessed superb skills, had tremendous balance and grace, he was athletic and he possessed a cannon of a shot from as far out as 35 yards. From the very moment Bobby made his United debut he was the ultimate professional. Always a gentleman on the pitch he never complained about crunching tackles and he never questioned the referee's decisions. In short, Bobby Charlton was the consummate professional footballer.

In 1973, when Bobby left Old Trafford after more than 750 appearances for the Reds, he became player-manager at Preston North End. He returned to United in 1984, where he remains a director, and a club ambassador.

On 3 April 2016, Old Trafford's South Stand was renamed the Sir Bobby Charlton Stand, in honour of the Manchester United legend.

DID YOU KNOW THAT?
Bobby and Jack Charlton made 141 appearances for England, a record which stood until it was passed Gary and Phil Neville.

For the Record
Born: 11 October 1937, Ashington, Northumberland
Country: England, 106 apps, 49 goals
Manchester United appearances: 758
Manchester United goals: 249
Manchester United debut: H v Charlton Athletic,
   6 October 1956, League

Duncan Edwards

There have been many polls over the last decade asking United fans "who is the greatest Manchester United player of all-time?" Legends such as Eric Cantona, Denis Law and George Best regularly appear in the Top 10 of fans' choices. However, to many United supporters the greatest player ever to pull on the red shirt of United was Duncan Edwards. Jimmy Murphy, assistant manager to Matt Busby, when asked about Duncan simply responded: "When I used to hear Muhammad Ali proclaim to the world that he was the greatest, I used to smile. You see the greatest of them all was an English footballer named Duncan Edwards."

Duncan made his Manchester United debut when he was aged just 16 years and 185 days, the youngest ever player in the English First Division at the time. He made his England debut in a 7–2 win over Scotland on 2 April 1955 at Wembley aged 18 years, 183 days becoming the youngest ever England international in the twentieth century, a record he held until 1998 when Michael Owen made his debut.

A young Duncan Edwards was first spotted when he played for his local team, Dudley Boys. Many teams were seeking Duncan's signature, but with the astute work of Murphy and Busby, he signed for United as an amateur in June 1952. He may have been only 15, but he was already a giant of a man, both in physical presence and stature.

An old-fashioned half-back (like a midfielder in today's football), Duncan had it all; presence, power, grace on the ball, composure, the ability to pass a ball with accuracy that would make an Olympic archer hang his head in disbelief, he scored goals (21 for United and 5 for England) but above all else, Duncan was a gentleman.

Speaking in July 2001 one of his teammates, Sir Bobby Charlton, said of Duncan: "Duncan Edwards is the one person who, even today, I really felt inferior to. I've never known anybody so gifted and strong and powerful with the presence that he had."

Who knows what Duncan, and indeed Manchester United, would have achieved had the Munich Air Disaster on 6 February 1958 not tragically claimed his life and those of seven of his team-mates. But the final words surely belong to Duncan himself. Despite a host of clubs clambering for his signature it turned out that Matt Busby and Jimmy Murphy did not need to use much persuasion to lure Duncan to Old Trafford. In his autobiography Matt Busby recalled Duncan saying to him: "I think Manchester United is the greatest team in the world. I'd give anything to play for you." Duncan was true to his word, he did give everything to United, including his life.

DID YOU KNOW THAT?
There is a statue of Duncan Edwards in his hometown of Dudley, and there is a street and a playing field named in his honour.

For the Record
Born: 1 October 1936, Dudley, West Midlands
Died: 21 February 1958, Munich, Germany
Country: England, 18 apps, 5 goals
Manchester United appearances: 177
Manchester United goals: 21
Manchester United debut: H v Cardiff City,
   4 April 1953, League

Sir Alex Ferguson, KBE, CBE

Sir Alex Ferguson broke records throughout his 28-year tenure as Manchester United manager. He won more trophies than any other manager in the history of English football, was in charge of Manchester United for more than 1,000 matches and was the club's longest serving manager; he transformed United into one of the world's biggest and most feared clubs. Just as Liverpool ruled in the 1970s and 1980s, the Reds dominated British football during the 1990s and 2000s with their brand of attractive, free-flowing, attacking style of football, a throwback to the glory days of George Best and Bobby Charlton.

However, it was not all plain sailing for Fergie. He was appointed United manager in succession to Ron Atkinson on 6 November 1986 and his first match in charge was against Oxford United at the Manor Ground. It was an inasuspicious start as relegation-threatened United went down 2–0. Fergie's teams improved, but there was no silverware to show for it. And, when United played an FA Cup tie at Nottingham Forest in January 1990, it was felt a defeat would signal the end of the for Fergie. They won 1–0, went on to lift the FA Cup, the Cup winners Cup and Football League Cup in successive seasons.

The League title remained elusive, but that all changed in season 1992–93, the first year of the FA Premier League. This time there were no slip-ups and when their closest rivals Aston Villa lost 1–0 to Oldham Athletic on 2 May 1993, United were champions for the first time since 1967. Having done it once, United wasted little time in repeating the feat a season later. When Chelsea were routed 4–0 in the FA Cup final, Fergie could add double-winner to his list of accomplishments.

United failed to make it three titles in a row in 1995, and were beaten in the FA Cup final too, but they returned to the top of the pile in 1996, and completed a second double into the bargain. All these great achievements almost paled into insignificance in 1999, when United not only won the Premier League and FA Cup again, they added the UEFA Champions League – their first for 31 years – and on what would have been Sir Matt Busby's 90th birthday.

Personal honours soon followed as a knighthood was bestowed on him. Sir Alex won two more championships in 2000 and 2001, becoming the first man to be in charge throughout three consecutive League title winning campaigns – a feat he would repeat 2007–09. In addition to his 13 League titles, Sir Alex was in charge for five FA Cup wins and a second UEFA Champions League success. It is probably safe to say that no manager or club will ever enjoy the level of success Sir Alex Ferguson brought to Manchester United.

On 5 November 2011, Old Trafford's North Stand was renamed as the Sir Alex Ferguson Stand, in his honour.

DID YOU KNOW THAT?

Sir Alex Ferguson is a racehorse owner and his best horse, Rock of Gibraltar, won more than £1 million in his career.

For the Record

Born: 31 December 1941 Glasgow, Scotland

Manchester United career: 1986–2013

League Titles: 1993, 1994, 1996, 1997, 1999, 2000, 2001, 2003, 2007, 2008, 2009, 2011, 2013

UEFA Champions League: 1999, 2008

FA Cup: 1990, 1994, 1996, 1999, 2004

European Cup winners Cup: 1991

League Cup: 1992, 2006, 2009, 2010

Ryan Giggs, OBE

Ryan Joseph Wilson was born on 29 November 1973 in Cardiff. To say that he had a magnificent career with Manchester United is a gross understatement; not only did he win more medals with United than any other player in the club's history but also his winners' medal haul – 13 Premier League, four FA Cup, two UEFA Champions League, World Club Championship, European Super Cup and four League Cup – makes him the most decorated British footballer ever. When he played in the 2008 UEFA Champions League Final, he passed Sir Bobby Charlton's United appearance record of 759.

Ryan joined United in 1990, signing professional forms later that year. In 1991 he adopted his mother's maiden name and became Ryan Giggs. He made his League debut in March 1991 against Everton at Old Trafford and two months later scored the only goal in a derby win over Manchester City. In October 1991, aged 17 years and 321 days, Ryan played for Wales against Germany, becoming Wales's youngest-ever full international. A month later he won his first medal as United beat Red Star Belgrade to take the European Super Cup. His first domestic medal arrived in March 1992, after United beat Nottingham Forest in the League Cup final, and he finished the season earning the PFA Young Player of the Year Award.

In 1992–93 Ryan won his first Premier League winners' medal and became the first two-time PFA Young Player of the Year. He was part of United's double-winning squads in both 1993–94 and 1995–96. A fourth Premiership medal in 1997 was the prelude to the unforgettable 1998–99 campaign. Ryan played a significant part in United's famous treble of Premiership, FA Cup and UEFA Champions League. On the way, Ryan scored what has since been voted the greatest goal in the history of the FA Cup in United's 2–1 FA Cup semi-final replay win over Arsenal. In November 1999 he won the World Club Championship against Palmeiras of Brazil in Tokyo. Two more Premiership titles followed in 2000 and 2001.

On 23 August 2002 he scored his 100th goal for United in a 2–2 draw at Chelsea. The following May, Ryan collected his eighth Premier League winners' medal and, a year later, a fourth FA Cup winners' meal was placed around his neck – in his native Cardiff – after Millwall had been beaten 3–0.

The one hole in his cv is international glory but, just as with George Best and Northern Ireland, Ryan did not play on the world stage because Wales failed to qualify for a major championship. Shortly after collecting his ninth Premiership medal Ryan won his 64th and final cap for Wales (scored 12 goals).

Giggs retired in 2014, after spending four matches as player-manager. He left Old Trafford when Jose Mourinho arrived as manager, having been Louis van Gaal's assisant.

DID YOU KNOW THAT?

Ryan's father, Danny Wilson, played rugby union for Cardiff and rugby league for Swinton and Wales.

For the Record

Born: 29 November 1973, Cardiff, Wales

Country: Wales, 64 apps, 12 goals

Manchester United appearances: 963

Manchester United goals: 168

Manchester United debut: H v Everton, 2 March 1991,

  League

Zlatan Ibrahimovic

On 1 July 2016, Zlatan Ibrahimovic, nicknamed "Ibracadabra," signed a one-year contract for Manchester United in a free transfer from Paris Saint-Germain, which had the option of being extended depending on his performance for the club. He was 34 years & 270 days old (born on 3 October 1981) when he put pen to paper for the Red Devils.

Many football pundits questioned Jose Mourinho's decision to sign a player who some sportswriters labelled a journeyman, having played for numerous clubs across Europe – Malmo, Ajax, Juventus, Inter Milan, Barcelona, AC Milan and Paris Saint-Germain where he won domestic and European trophies galore. But Jose had worked with Ibrahimovic during his tenure in charge of Inter Milan (2008–10) and he knew first hand what the Big Swede (116 caps for Sweden 2001–16, 62 goals) could bring to the table. Namely a fantastically gifted footballer – tall (standing 6ft 5in) strong and agile, a great header of the ball, adept with either foot and renowned for his overhead kicks and other spectacular strikes.

Zlatan made his competitive Manchester United debut in a 2–1 win over the Premier League's fairy tale 2015–16 Champions, Leicester City, in the FA Community Shield on Sunday 7 August 2016. He netted the winner in the 83rd minute at Wembley Stadium. In his Premier League debut for United one week later, he scored with a long-range strike in a 3–1 away win at AFC Bournemouth. On 20 August 2016, he made his Old Trafford debut and scored both goals, a header in the first half and a penalty in the second, in a 2–0 victory over Southampton. Zlatan became the ninth player to score in his first three games for United, and the first since Ian Storey-Moore in season 1971–72.

In early November, he again scored twice in a 3–1 away win against Swansea City; on 5 February 2017, Ibrahimovi became the oldest player to manage at least 15 goals in a single Premier League season at the age of 35 years and 125 days, when he netted during Manchester United's 3–0 victory at Leicester City. Little more than a week later he notched his first Manchester United hat-trick in a 3–0 win over Saint-Étienne in the Europa League and at the end of the month he scored another brace (a free-kick and a header) to clinch United's victory in the 2017 League Cup Final.

Sadly, a serious knee injury sustained in late April ruled him out for the remainder of the season, but in the space of 10 short months, the Swede became a United legend – netting a remarkable 28 goals and becoming an instant hero to the fans. Zlatan was released by United on 30 June 2017.

DID YOU KNOW THAT?

Like his Manchester United predecessor, David Beckham, Ibrahimovic is a body art enthusiast. His range of tattoos include depictions of a feather, a Koi fish, an Ace of Hearts and the legend "Only God can judge me" emblazoned on his ribcage.

For the Record

Born: 3 October 1981, Malmo, Sweden

Country: Sweden, 116 apps, 62 goals

Manchester United appearances: 46

Manchester United goals: 28

Manchester United debut: v Leicester City, 7 August 2016, FA Community Shield, Wembley Stadium

---

Roy Keane

Roy Maurice Keane was born in Cork, Republic of Ireland, on 10 August 1971 and began his football career at Rockmount FC in Cork. "Fail to prepare, prepare to fail" is a line from Roy's autobiography simply entitled *Keane*, and this just about summed up his playing career. Roy was a warrior on the pitch as he took the battle to the opposition, leading from the front. He was outspoken, aggressive, often controversially so, powerful and never shirked a tackle, a true midfield general who was the driving force of Manchester United's midfield for 12 years from 1993 to 2005.

Few players can say that they played for two legends of football management, but Keano can. In 1989, Roy signed as a semi-professional with Cobh Ramblers, before joining Brian Clough's Nottingham Forest for £20,000. At the end of the 1992–93 season, Forest were relegated and despite overtures from a number of clubs Roy joined Alex Ferguson's inaugural FA Premier League winners, Manchester United, a re-emerging force in British football, for a club record transfer fee of £3.75 million.

In his first season at Old Trafford, Roy was part of the United team which completed the Premier League and FA Cup double, a feat that the team repeated two seasons later. After winning a third Premiership winner's medal in four seasons at the club in 1997, following the shock retirement of Eric Cantona, Roy was appointed United captain. However, he missed much of the next season with a knee injury. However, United's inspirational captain returned for the 1998–99 season and he led the side to the unprecedented treble, which included a superhuman performance from Roy against Juventus in the UEFA Champions League semi-final.

Unfortunately for him, Roy was shown a yellow card against Juventus and thus was suspended for United's dramatic 2–1 win over Bayern Munich in the final. In 2000, he was recognised by his fellow professionals, winning the PFA Players' Player of the Year Award.

Roy captained United to nine major honours, making him the club's most successful captain, but also was sent off 11 times in his Old Trafford career. In 2005, Keano set a new record by appearing in his seventh FA Cup final (one with Forest). All in all, in his 12 seasons at United, Roy won seven FA Premier League titles, four FA Cups and the Intercontinental Cup.

At full international level, Roy played for the Republic of Ireland 67 times, although his international career may be best remembered for a spat with coach Mick McCarthy before the 2002 World Cup finals.

In November 2005 Keano left United and, a month later, fulfilled a boyhood dream by joining Glasgow Celtic, but retired after the 2005–06 season.

DID YOU KNOW THAT?
Growing up in Cork, Roy trained as a boxer and had four bouts – of course, he won all of them.

For the Record
Born: 10 August 1971, Cork, Republic of Ireland
Country: Republic of Ireland, 67 apps, 9 goals
Manchester United appearances: 480
Manchester United goals: 51
Manchester United debut: N v Arsenal, 7 August 1993,
   FA Charity Shield

Denis Law

In July 1962 Matt Busby paid a British record transfer fee of £115,000 to sign Denis Law from the Italian club, Torino. The legendary Bill Shankly, when he was in charge at Huddersfield Town in 1956, signed Law as a 16-year-old straight from school in Aberdeen. Denis played for Huddersfield and then moved on to Manchester City.

On 28 January 1961, Denis had the misfortune to score six goals in an FA Cup fourth round tie for City against Luton Town – only for it to be abandoned, so the feat was wiped from the record books and, to make matters worse, Luton won the tie when it was replayed. Torino signed Denis from City in 1961, but he spent only one season in Italy before Busby brought him back to England. On his debut for United he scored in a 2–2 draw with West Bromwich Albion and, at the end of his first season at Old Trafford, he won the FA Cup with United at Wembley in May 1963 scoring in the final.

Denis was the supreme goal-poacher with razor-sharp reflexes. "The King", as the Stretford End affectionately dubbed him, was as brave as a lion, as cunning as a fox and he seemed to possess the ability to leap in the air like a salmon out of water. No United fan, or indeed football fan that ever saw him play, could ever forget his trademark goal celebration with his right arm raised high in the air clutching his sleeve.

In 1964 Denis was voted European Footballer of the Year but sadly his bravery in battle cost him a place in United's 1968 European Cup final side. On that famous night against Benfica at Wembley, Denis was lying in hospital, recovering from a knee operation. Although he was not at the stadium when United were crowned European champions, make no mistake about it, Denis had played a major part in getting the Reds to the final at Wembley.

In 1973 Denis was sensationally placed on the transfer list by United manager, Tommy Docherty. He returned to Manchester City where few will forget his back-heeled goal in the Manchester derby at Old Trafford on 27 April 1974. Denis did not celebrate his goal, merely walking away with his head bowed, the thought that he may have condemned United to the Second Division apparent on his face. Shortly afterwards he was substituted and a pitch invasion caused the referee to abandon the match with City leading 1–0. The other results went against United, and they were relegated. After the game, Denis never kicked another football in English football again.

George Best once said of Denis: "He's up there with the all-time greats. Electric. He'd snap up any half chance. As a bloke and as a pal, he's a different class. Nobody has a bad word about Denis."

DID YOU KNOW THAT?

Although Denis missed the European Cup final through injury he got to hold the cup the next day when Matt Busby and his team-mates visited him in hospital.

For the Record

Born: 24 February 1940, Aberdeen, Scotland

Country: Scotland, 55 apps, 30 goals

Manchester United appearances: 404

Manchester United goals: 237

Manchester United debut: H v West Bromwich Albion, 18 August 1962, League

---

Bryan Robson, OBE

Ask any Manchester United fan what they thought the chance of winning a game without Bryan Robson in the side and they would have said: "Not very good." That is how key Robbo was to The Red Devils after he signed for the club in 1975. Much as Bobby Charlton a decade or so before him, during his time at United Robbo became recognised as "Mr United."

Bryan was born on 11 January 1957 in Chester-le-Street, County Durham and grew up supporting Newcastle United. He had trials with Burnley, Coventry City, Newcastle, Sheffield Wednesday and West Bromwich Albion, but only the Baggies took a chance on the skinny 15-year-old, and Don Howe signed him in the summer of 1972. It was certainly a gamble as, at the time, Bryan stood just 5 feet 2 inches tall and weighed only 7 stones. Howe put Robbo on a diet of raw eggs and Guinness to help build him up, but the unusual diet obviously worked and, in 1974, Bryan signed professional terms, going on to make his first team debut on 12 April 1975 in a 3–1 away win at York City.

He played more than 200 times for West Brom before, in October 1981, Ron Atkinson, his former Baggies boss, broke the British transfer record fee by paying £1.5 million to bring him to Old Trafford. The move was questioned, mainly because of Bryan's inury record: he had suffered three leg breaks during the 1976–77 season. But, over the course of the next 13 years, he displayed an insatiable will to win, combined with drive, motivation, power, skill and tenacity, all of which made him the ultimate box-to-box player and he achieved legendary status among the Old Trafford and England faithful.

At the start of the 1982–83 season Robbo replaced Ray Wilkins as United's skipper and held the role until he left Old

Trafford 12 seasons later, making him the longest serving captain in the club's history. "Captain Marvel", as he quickly became to be known, was the driving force behind Atkinson's team which tried in vain to break Liverpool"s dominance of the Football League during the late 1970s and early 1980s.

Robbo and Atkinson had their moments, with Captain Marvel leading United to FA Cup glory in 1983 and 1985. Alex Ferguson, who replaced Atkinson in 1986, built a new side around the ever dependable Robson and after winning a third FA Cup winners' medal in 1990, the European Cup Winners' Cup in 1991, UEFA Super Cup in 1991, League Cup in 1992, Bryan helped lead United to their first Championship success in 26 years. Standing beside Steve Bruce he lifted the inaugural Premier League trophy before an ecstatic and thunderous Old Trafford crowd on 3 May 1993.

Bryan's last game for United was on 8 May 1994, a 0–0 draw with Coventry City, after which he collected his second Championship winner's medal. He left Old Trafford on 31 May 1994 to become player-manager at Middlesbrough.

DID YOU KNOW THAT?

Bryan Robson's Captain Marvel nickname was taken from a comic book superhero created by artist CC Beck in 1939.

For the Record

Born: 11 January 1957, Chester-le-Street, Durham

Country: England, 90 apps, 26 goals

Manchester United appearances: 461

Manchester United goals: 99

Manchester United debut: A v Tottenham Hotspur, 7 October 1981, Football League Cup

Cristiano Ronaldo

Cristiano Ronaldo dos Santos Aveiro was born on 5 February 1985 in Funchal, on the Portuguese island of Madeira. He joined his first team in 1993, Andorinha – where his father was kit manager. At the age of 10 he signed for CD National and, at 15, helped them to the Portuguese Second Division title. Ronaldo went on a three-day trial with Sporting Clube of Lisbon, who quickly signed him. He scored twice on his debut against Moreirense. His big break came in 2003, when Manchester United played Sporting in a friendly and the players were so impressed with Ronaldo's display on both wings – Sporting won 3-1 – that they urged Sir Alex to buy him. Having just lost David Beckham to Real Madrid, United paid Sporting £12.24m for Ronaldo's services.

On arriving at Old Trafford he asked for squad number 28, his number at Sporting, but Sir Alex handed him the No.7 shirt, a number made famous by George Best and Beckham. Ronaldo made his debut for Manchester United on the opening day of the 2003–04 Premier League season, coming on as a substitute against Bolton Wanderers at Old Trafford. United were leading 1–0 at the time and within minutes, he had won a penalty, which Ruud van Nistelrooy had saved. Ronaldo didn't score, but United did add another three goals, the first coming from his cross, to win 4–0. In his first season at United Ronaldo appeared in 39 matches and scored six goals, including one in the FA Cup final victory over Millwall. Over the next two seasons, he netted 21 goals in 97 games and was named FIFPro Special Young Player of the Year in 2005 and 2006.

As good as he had been in his first three seasons at Old Trafford, Ronaldo took his game to new levels in 2006–07. His 23 goals from 52 matches in all competitions played a big part in United's ninth Premiership crown. He also won two Barclays Player of the Month Awards, the PFA Young Player of the Year, PFA Players' Player of the Year, Football Writers' Association Player of the Year, 2006 Portuguese Sports Personality of the Year and 2007 Portuguese Player of the Year awards. Amazingly, Ronaldo had an even better 2007–08 campaign, scoring 42 goals in all competitions as United swept to a second straight Premier League title and won the UEFA Champions League. He also retained his individual Barclays, FWA, Manchester United and PFA Player of the Year awards.

UEFA, FIFPro and FIFA recognised Ronaldo's outstanding contributions in 2008 naming him their player of the year. In 2008–09, United won a third consecutive Premier League title, were runners-up in the Champions League and won the FA World Club Championship. Ronaldo contributed 25 goals to the cause. Unsurprisingly, Real Madrid – with Florentino Perez back as club president – were desperate to sign him and, in June 2009, the Spanish giants smashed the world transfer record when they splashed out £80 million to get their man.

DID YOU KNOW THAT?
Cristiano Ronaldo's parents named him after the former US President, Ronald Reagan.

For the Record
Born: 5 February 1985, Funchal, Madeira, Portugal
Country: Portugal, 138 apps, 71 goals
Manchester United appearances: 292
Manchester United goals: 118
Manchester United debut: H v Bolton Wanderers,
   16 August 2003, League

Wayne Rooney

Wayne Rooney was born on 24 October 1985 in Liverpool. He grew up on Merseyside supporting Everton, and, aged 16 years and 297 days, made his debut for the Toffees. Two months later Wayne became the youngest ever goalscorer in the history of the FA Premier League when he fired a long-range effort in against Arsenal at Goodison Park.

Sven-Goran Erikkson gave him his England debut in February 2003 aged 17 years and 11 days, and he went on to be a star at the Euro 2004 international tournament.

In the aftermath of his outstanding displays in Portugal, Rooney joined Manchester United in a deal worth around £31 million. Aged 18, he was the world's most expensive teenager. On 28 September, following his recovery from the foot injury he sustained during Euro 2004, Wayne made his United debut at Old Trafford against Fenerbahce in the UEFA Champions League. The Manchester United faithful instantly took him to their hearts when he scored a hat-trick and laid on another goal in United's 6–2 thrashing of the Turks.

In February 2006, Wayne collected his first winner's medal as a professional when United took Wigan Athletic apart in the Carling Cup final at the Millennium Stadium. His two goals in the 4–0 win earned him the Man of the Match award.

Wayne has won almost everything there is to win as a United player, including three consecutive Premier League titles, the UEFA Champions League, three League Cups and the FIFA World Club Championship. On a personal level, his honours include: PFA Young Player of the Year in 2005 and 2006; FIFPro World Young Player of the Year in 2005; Football Writers Association Footballer of the Year 2010 and PFA Player of the Year 2010.

A brief spat with Sir Alex in October 2010 was settled when Wayne signed a new contract taking him up to 2015. Wayne won his fourth and fifth Premier League winners' medals with United in seasons 2010–11 and 2012–13 and in season 2015–16, he captained Manchester United to FA Cup success with a 2–1 extra time win over Crystal Palace.

Wayne has set all sorts of records for England. On 8 September 2015, he broke Sir Bobby Charlton's goal-scoring record, netting his 50th in a 2–0 UEFA Euro 2016 qualifying defeat of Switzerland. A year later, Wayne's 116th cap, a 1–0 win in Slovakia, made him England's most-capped outfield player, and second in appearances behind Peter Shilton.

On 21 January 2017, Wayne scored with a free-kick against Stoke City to register his 250th Manchester United goal to pass Sir Bobby's Charlton's old record. When Wayne come on as a 90th-minute substitute in the 2017 UEFA Europa League final, it was his fourth appearance in a major European final for Manchester United, equalling the record held by Ryan Giggs.

DID YOU KNOW THAT?

On 6 September 2003, against Macedonia, Wayne became England's youngest ever goalscorer, aged 17 years, 317 days.

For the Record
Born: 24 October 1985, Liverpool
Country: England, 119 apps, 53 goals
Manchester United appearances: 559
Manchester United goals: 253
Manchester United debut: H v Fenerbahce,
28 September 2004, UEFA Champions League

Paul Scholes

Paul Scholes was born on 16 November 1974 in Salford. Aged just 14 he began training with Manchester United and signed as a trainee on 8 July 1991 after he left the Cardinal Langley Roman Catholic High School in Middleton. Paul was one of Fergie's Fledglings, the group of players which included Ryan Giggs, David Beckham, Nicky Butt and Gary and Phil Neville.

He turned professional on 23 July 1993 and was given the squad number 24. On 21 September 1994, Paul made his debut scoring twice in a 2–1 League Cup win at Port Vale and, three days later, he made his Premier League debut at Ipswich Town. In 1995–96 Fergie's Fledglings stormed the Premier League, this after Alan Hansen's infamous "You'll never win anything with kids" quote on the BBC's *Match of the Day* programme following United's 3–1 opending day loss at Aston Villa. Paul helped United to become the first English team to win the double of League and FA Cup twice. A season later, now in the No.18 shirt, he won a second League winner's medal.

During United's unprecedented treble-winning season of 1998–99, the "Ginger Prince" was a cornerstone of the all-conquering side, although suspension ruled him out of the UEFA Champions League Final. A fourth Premier League champion's medal followed in season 1999–2000, and number five came a year later. Paul scored a career-high 20 goals in all competitions in 2002–03, the season United regained the Premier League title.

On 22 October 2006, he celebrated becoming the ninth United player to appear in 500 matches for the the club, scoring in a 2–0 Premier League win against Liverpool. Paul played a pivotal role in the heart of the midfield which saw United dominate the Premiership, winning the title in 2007, 2008 and 2009.

The records and honours kept coming for this loyal one-club man: in September 2008, Paul was inducted into the English Football Hall of Fame; on 22 April 2009, it was the 600th United appearance; on 6 March 2010, he became the 19th player to score 100 Premier League goals (also the third United player to do so after Ryan Giggs and Wayne Rooney); and, on 22 August 2010, Paul scored his 150th club goal.

Such was his devotion to United that Paul decided to call time on a very successful England career in 2004, after 66 caps and 14 goals, to prolong his club career, which eventually ended in 2013. He is unassuming, rarely appears on TV screens, but will always be held in great esteem by United's fans who recognise what he did for his club and that he did it wearing his United heart on his sleeve.

Sir Bobby Charlton once summed up Paul: "He's always so in control and pinpoint accurate with his passing – a beautiful player to watch."

DID YOU KNOW THAT?
Paul Scholes was the first player ever to score against both Inter Milan (1999) and AC Milan (2010) at the San Siro in the Champions League.

For the Record
Born: 16 October 1974, Salford, Manchester
Country: England, 66 apps, 14 goals
Manchester United appearances: 718
Manchester United goals: 155
Manchester United debut: A v Port Vale,
 21 September 1994, League Cup

CHAPTER

4

MANCHESTER UNITED
FANTASY TEAMS

Everyone has their all-time favourite player and, if pushed, everyone also will come up with their all-time favourite 11. One of the best games to play when you are on a long trip to a match is to pick your fantasy team, your dream Manchester United 11 to take on the world.

What follows, here, is a selection of 10 United fantasy teams on a variety of themes. When you look through them, you will be sure to think of many players who would be in your starting 11, or one of the seven substitutes and you would be right. It is the essential beauty of a fantasy team; you can never be proved wrong in your choice.

These are fantasy teams taken from United's long and storied history, so your Sir Bobby Charlton would not be the 73-year-old United legend, but the 30-year-old World and European Cup winner. Anyone old enough to remember the Busby Babes may say that those players were the greatest, but a few generations earlier, there was the team starring Billy Meredith, the Wayne Rooney of his era.

Why not take it a stage further and pick a fantasy team in which every player starts with the same letter. Who would come out on top? The Beckham/Best Bs, Cantona/Charlton Cs. Rooney/Ronaldo Rs? The argument is already starting!

MUFC International XI

1
Peter
SCHMEICHEL

2
John
SIVEBAEK

6
Jaap
STAM

5
Nemanja
VIDIC

3
Patrice
EVRA

7
Cristiano
RONALDO

8
Arnold
MUHREN

4
Robin
VAN PERSIE

11
Andrei
KANCHELSKIS

9
Ruud
VAN NISTELROOY

10
Eric
CANTONA

Substitutes

Fabien *BARTHEZ*, Nikola *JOVANOVIC, PARK* Ji-sung,

NANI, ANDERSON, Jesper *OLSEN*, Zlatan *IBRAHIMOVIC*

Manager

Sir Alex *FERGUSON* CBE

DID YOU KNOW THAT?

Goalkeeper Peter Schmeichel was invited by the BBC to select the top five goals scored in the Premier League and FA Cup during March 2005 for their "Goal of the Month" competition on *Match of the Day*. Schmeichel's choices came as something of a surprise to the programme's production team because not a single viewer agreed with his selection of the three best goals – a unique outcome in the history of the competition on the long-running football highlights show.

MUFC Scotland XI

1
Jim
LEIGHTON

2
Stewart
HOUSTON

6
Martin
BUCHAN

5
Gordon
McQUEEN

3
Arthur
ALBISTON

7
Gordon
STRACHAN

8
Jim
McCALLIOG

4
Paddy
CRERAND

11
Willie
MORGAN

9
Brian
McCLAIR

10
Denis
LAW

Substitutes

Andy *GORAM*, Alex *FORSYTH*, Jim *HOLTON*, Francis *BURNS*,

Darren *FLETCHER*, Lou *MACARI*, Joe *JORDAN*,

Manager

Sir Matt *BUSBY*

DID YOU KNOW THAT?

Three Manchester United managers also managed the Scottish national team: Sir Matt Busby, Tommy Docherty and Sir Alex Ferguson.

DID YOU KNOW THAT?

Central defender Martin Buchan has a unique place in British football as he is the only man to have captained the winners of both the Scottish FA Cup and the FA Cup. He led Aberdeen to glory in 1970 and United in 1977.

MUFC England XI

1
Alex **STEPNEY**

2
Roger **BYRNE**

6
Duncan **EDWARDS**

5
Rio **FERDINAND**

3
Bill **FOULKES**

7
Bryan **ROBSON**

8
Johnny **BERRY**

4
Nobby **STILES**

11
David **PEGG**

9
Bobby **CHARLTON**

10
Wayne **ROONEY**

Substitutes

Gary **BAILEY**, Eddie **COLMAN**, Mark **JONES**, Steve **COPPELL**,
Dennis **VIOLLET**, David **BECKHAM**, Tommy **TAYLOR**

Manager

Ron **ATKINSON**

DID YOU KNOW THAT?

Walter Winterbottom, a Manchester United half back from 1936 to 1938, managed England from 1946 to 1962, guiding them to four successive World Cup finals tournaments.

DID YOU KNOW THAT?

Rio Ferdinand was appointed England captain early in 2010 and was in line to lead England into the World Cup finals in South Africa. Unfortunately, a knee injury meant he had to withdraw from the tournament just before it opened.

MUFC Republic of Ireland XI

1
Paddy *ROCHE*

2
Johnny *CAREY*

6
Kevin *MORAN*

5
Paul *McGRATH*

3
Denis *IRWIN*

7
Johnny *GILES*

8
Roy *KEANE*

4
Gerry *DALY*

11
Ashley *GRIMES*

9
Frank *STAPLETON*

10
Liam *WHELAN*

Substitutes

Billy *BEHAN*, Shay *BRENNAN*, Tony *DUNNE*, Noel *CANTWELL*,

Mick *MARTIN*, Darron *GIBSON*, Don *GIVENS*

Manager

Frank *O'FARRELL*

DID YOU KNOW THAT?

Johnny Carey, who captained Manchester United to FA Cup success in 1948 and the League Championship in 1952, won seven caps for Northern Ireland and 29 for the Republic of Ireland.

DID YOU KNOW THAT?

Paul McGrath was actually born in the London suburb of Ealing, though he grew up in Dublin. Scout Billy Behan saw Paul play as a youngster and alerted United to him.

MUFC Northern Ireland XI

Substitutes

Roy **CARROLL**, Jonny **EVANS**, Corey **EVANS**, Tommy **SLOAN**,
Davd **HEALY**, Chris **McGRATH**, Tommy **JACKSON**

Manager

Bob **BISHOP**

DID YOU KNOW THAT?

Harry Gregg was on the plane returning from United's European Cup game against Red Star Belgrade when it crashed in Munich in 1958. Harry survived and was one of the first to help people from the wreckage as it lay on the runway at Munich Airport.

DID YOU KNOW THAT?

Aged 17 years and 41 days in 1982, Norman Whiteside was the youngest player ever to appear in the World Cup finals.

MUFC Wales XI

1
William
JOHN

2
John
POWELL

6
Thomas
BURKE

5
Samuel
BENNION

3
Roger
DOUGHTY

7
Billy
MEREDITH

8
Mickey
THOMAS

4
Clayton
BLACKMORE

11
Ryan
GIGGS

9
Ron
DAVIES

10
Mark
HUGHES

Substitutes

Wyn *DAVIES*, John *DOUGHTY*, John *OWEN*, Colin *WEBSTER*,
Robbie *SAVAGE*, Alan *DAVIES*, David *WILLIAMS*

Manager

Jimmy *MURPHY*

DID YOU KNOW THAT?

Jimmy Murphy, Manchester United's assistant manager, missed the fateful European Cup trip to Red Star Belgrade in February 1958 because, as the manager of Wales, he was preparing the team for a forthcoming international against Israel in Cardiff. Jimmy was put in charge of United while Matt Busby recovered from the injuries he sustained in the Munich air crash, and he guided the Reds to the 1958 FA Cup final as well as leading Wales to the 1958 World Cup finals in Sweden.

MUFC Premier League XI

1
Peter
SCHMEICHEL

2
Gary
NEVILLE

5
Rio
FERDINAND

4
Gary
PALLISTER

3
Denis
IRWIN

7
Paul
SCHOLES

6
Roy
KEANE

11
Ryan
GIGGS

9
Cristiano
RONALDO

10
Eric
CANTONA

8
Wayne
ROONEY

Substitutes

Edwin **VAN DER SAR**, Steve **BRUCE**, David **BECKHAM**,

Mark **HUGHES**, Ruud **VAN NISTELROOY**

Manager

Sir Alex **FERGUSON**, CBE

DID YOU KNOW THAT?

When France failed to qualify for the 1994 World Cup finals, Cantona and David Ginola were made the scapegoats by the French FA, and neither were ever picked again. At both Euro 2004 and the 2006 World Cup, Eric supported England and not France.

DID YOU KNOW THAT?

Ryan Giggs is the only player to have won 13 Premier League titles.

MUFC 2010 & 2014 World Cup XI

1
David
DA GEA
Spain (2014)

2
Antonio
VALENCIA
Ecuador (2014)

5
Chris
SMALLING
England (2014)

4
Phil
JONES
England (2014)

3
Patrice
EVRA
France (2014)

8
Michael
CARRICK
England (2010)

6
Marouane
FELLAINE
Belgium (2014)

7
NANI
Portugal (2014)

9
Wayne
ROONEY
England (2010)

10
Javier
HERNANDEZ
Mexico (2014)

11
Juan
MATA
Spain (2014)

Substitutes

Sergio **ROMERO** (Argentina, 2014), Adnan **JANUZAJ** (Belgium, 2014),

Tom **CLEVERLEY** (England, 2014), Shinji **KAGAWA** (Japan, 2014),

Danny **WELBECK** (England, 2014), Robin **VAN PERSIE** (Netherlands, 2014)

Manager

Louis **VAN GAAL** (Netherlands, 2014)

DID YOU KNOW THAT?

United and Chelsea led the way among Premier League clubs with 16 players each in the squads for the 32 finalists.

DID YOU KNOW THAT?

Louis Van Gaal was announced as the new Manchester United manager on 19 May 2014, but he did not take over until the middle of July as he was in charge of the Dutch team which finished third in the FIFA World Cup in Brazil.

MUFC/Leeds United XI

1
Chris
TURNER

2
Brian
GREENHOFF

6
Gordon
McQUEEN

5
Rio
FERDINAND

3
Denis
IRWIN

7
Lee
SHARPE

8
Gordon
STRACHAN

4
Johnny
GILES

11
Peter
BARNES

9
Joe
JORDAN

10
Eric
CANTONA

Substitutes

Mickey **THOMAS**, Jimmy **GREENHOFF**, Andy **RITCHIE**,

Alan **SMITH**, David **HEALY**

Player-Manager

Gordon **STRACHAN** OBE

DID YOU KNOW THAT?

Johnny Giles won an FA Cup winners' medal with Manchester United in 1963 and an FA Cup winners' medal with Leeds United in 1972. Gordon Strachan won an FA Cup winners' medal with Manchester United in 1985 and the First Division Championship with Leeds United in 1992.

DID YOU KNOW THAT?

Leeds United caused a massive FA Cup shock in January 2010 when they beat United 1–0 at Old Trafford in round three.

MUFC/Manchester City XI

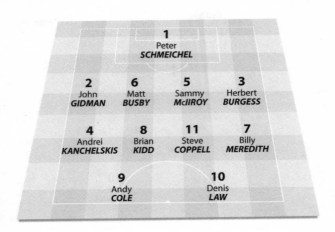

1
Peter
SCHMEICHEL

2
John
GIDMAN

6
Matt
BUSBY

5
Sammy
McILROY

3
Herbert
BURGESS

4
Andrei
KANCHELSKIS

8
Brian
KIDD

11
Steve
COPPELL

7
Billy
MEREDITH

9
Andy
COLE

10
Denis
LAW

Substitutes
Tony **COTON**, Wyn **DAVIES**, Peter **BARNES**,
Sandy **TURNBULL**, Carlos **TEVEZ**

Manager
Ernest **MANGNALL**

DID YOU KNOW THAT?

Sir Matt Busby won the FA Cup three times, once as a player and twice as a manager. A year after being on the losing side as City went down 3–0 to Everton, Busby – who played at wing-half – collected a winner's medal when Portsmouth were defeated 2–1. Busby's first major trophy as a manager came in the 1948 FA Cup final, when United beat Blackpool 4–2. After a 15-year wait, Busby again tasted FA Cup glory as Leicester City were downed 3–1. United also lost two FA Cup finals, to Aston Villa in 1957 and Bolton Wanderers in 1958.

CHAPTER

5

UP FOR
THE CUP

"Glory, glory Man United," the chant has reverberated around some of the biggest stadiums in the country after the Reds have picked up silverware. In fact, no club has won as many major cup finals (FA Cup and Football League Cup) as United. Red ribbons have adorned the FA Cup on 12 occasions and the Football League Cup, in all of its various guises five times, to say nothing of the 21 FA Charity/Community Shield triumphs (four of which were shared).

United have been winning cups on a regular basis since the 1940s, but the first time was back in the early years of the last century. And of course, this cup glory says nothing of the 20 Football League/Premier League championships which have gone United's way and the more than half-dozen UEFA and FIFA club cup successes.

All the domestic cup final victories are described over the next few pages, from that 1909 FA Cup defeat of Bristol City to the 2017 League Cup Final victory over Southampton. And for the statistics fan, every one of the United line-ups in each final – and replay – is given, together with the substitutes. To conclude the section, there is review of the FA Charity/Community Shield. It is not a knock-out competition, but it remains a major annual event on the English football calendar.

FA Cup 1909

Both teams were making their FA Cup final debuts and because the two sides wore red shirts, the FA instructed them to wear a change of strip. United wore white shirts with a red "V". A record crowd of 70,000 turned up at the Crystal Palace to see United win the Cup thanks to a goal from Sandy Turnbull, after a shot from Harry Halse had hit the crossbar. Charlie Roberts had the honour of becoming the first Manchester United player to lift the FA Cup.

FA CUP FINAL

24 APRIL 1909, THE CRYSTAL PALACE, Att. 71,401

Manchester United (1) **1**   v   **Bristol City** (0) **0**

A. Turnbull

Manchester United: Moger, Stacey, Hayes, Duckworth,

Roberts, Bell, Meredith, Halse, J. Turnbull,

A. Turnbull, Wall

DID YOU KNOW THAT?

Sandy Turnbull had been struggling with an injury in the run-up to the final. Manager Ernest Mangnall needed persuading to pick him and it came from skipper Charlie Roberts, who reportedly said, "[Turnbull] might get a goal and if he does we can afford to carry him."

DID YOU KNOW THAT?

With Sandy Turnbull less than fully fit, the last thing United needed – in the days before substitutes – was to have another player go down. But this is what happened to left-back Vince Hayes. After receiving lengthy treatment, he returned but could only play as a forward.

FA Cup 1948

Thirty-nine years after making their first FA Cup final appearance, United were at Wembley for the 1948 final. The Blackpool side, which included great players such as Stanley Matthews and Stan Mortensen, took the lead in the 12th minute when Eddie Shimwell scored from the penalty spot. In the 28th minute Jack Rowley levelled the scores, only for Mortensen to put Blackpool 2–1 up at half-time. In the second half United managed to shackle Matthews and thereby control the Blackpool attack. In the 69th minute Jack Rowley made the score 2–2, and shortly afterwards Stan Pearson put United ahead for the first time in the game. With only seven minutes of the match remaining, John Anderson's cross ended up in the back of the Blackpool net, thanks to a deflection off Blackpool's Hugh Kelly. United captain Johnny Carey collected the Cup from King George VI.

FA CUP FINAL
24 APRIL 1948, WEMBLEY STADIUM, Att. 99,000

Manchester United (1) **4**   v   **Blackpool** (2) **2**

Rowley (2), Pearson,   Shimwell (pen), Mortensen
Anderson

Manchester United: Crompton, Carey, Aston, Anderson,
Chilton, Cockburn, Delaney, Morris,
Rowley, Pearson, Mitten

DID YOU KNOW THAT?
Matt Busby won his first trophy at the end of his third season as Manchester United boss; it was also United's first FA Cup final at Wembley, which had first staged the final in 1923.

FA Cup 1963

United reached the 1963 FA Cup final despite having spent most of the season fighting a rearguard action against the possibility of relegation. Their opponents, Leicester City, were clear favourites to lift the trophy, having finished fourth in Division One. In the 29th minute, "The King", Denis Law, opened the scoring with a fine turn and shot inside the box, which Leicester and England goalkeeper, Gordon Banks, could do nothing about. Twelve minutes into the second half David Herd, whose father played alongside Matt Busby for Manchester City in the 1933 and 1934 FA Cup finals, made it 2–0 to the Reds. With ten minutes remaining, Ken Keyworth pulled a goal back for Leicester to give them a glimmer of hope. A couple of minutes later, however, Herd grabbed his second, and United's third, goal of the game to ensure the Cup was going back to Old Trafford for the first time since 1948.

FA CUP FINAL
25 MAY 1963, WEMBLEY STADIUM, Att. 100,000

Manchester United (1) **3**　　v　　**Leicester City** (0) **1**

Herd (2), Law　　　　　　　Keyworth

Manchester United: Gaskell, Dunne, Cantwell, Crerand,

Foulkes, Setters, Giles, Quixall,

Herd, Law, Charlton

DID YOU KNOW THAT?
In the third round Denis Law scored a hat-trick in a 5–0 win over the club where he began his professional career – Huddersfield Town. In total Denis scored six goals in United's six Cup ties.

FA Cup 1977

In 1977, Liverpool, already League champions, were out to emulate the Arsenal team of 1971 by winning the Double of Championship and FA Cup in the same season; they had also reached the final of the European Cup. But this United team were out to prove that the previous year's defeat in the Cup final, at the hands of Southampton, was just a mere blip. While United's Arthur Albiston was making his FA Cup debut, Liverpool's Kevin Keegan was playing his last game for the club before his move to SV Hamburg in West Germany. In the first half Liverpool played their possession game, but they could not break down a United defence marshalled superbly by Martin Buchan. The game came to life in a five-minute period in the second half that brought three goals. Stuart Pearson fired United into the lead only for the old 1970s cliche of "Liverpool are at their most dangerous when they are behind" to come true, Jimmy Case levelling for the Merseysiders. However, thanks to a deflected goal off Jimmy Greenhoff from Lou Macari's shot, United won the Cup. Tommy Docherty's promise to the United fans in May 1976 that United would be back at Wembley the following year to win the Cup was kept. Sadly for many United fans, this was Docherty's last game in charge of the Reds, since he was sacked by the club six weeks later.

FA CUP FINAL

21 MAY 1977, WEMBLEY STADIUM, Att. 100,000

Manchester United (0) **2**   v   **Liverpool** (0) **1**

Pearson, J. Greenhoff   Case

Manchester United: Stepney, Nicholl, Albiston, McIlroy,

B. Greenhoff, Buchan, Coppell, J. Greenhoff,

Pearson, Macari, Hill (McCreery)

FA Cup 1983

There is an adage in football that the underdog has got only once chance to cause an upset, and that was proved true in the 1983 FA Cup final. It was felt that Brighton & Hove Albion, already relegated from the First Division, were along for the ride. But they gave United a terrible fright. Gordon Smith gave them a half-time lead before Frank Stapleton equalised and Ray Wilkins scored a wonder-goal to make it 2–1 to United. But Gary Stevens forced extra time, in the last minute of which Gary Bailey made a miraculous save to deny Smith the winner and secure a replay.

In a one-sided replay, Bryan Robson scored first for the Reds after 25 minutes. Five minutes later, Norman Whiteside added a second and Robson netted number three after 44 minutes. When United were awarded a second-half penalty, Robson unselfishly let Arnold Muhren score from the spot.

FA CUP FINAL

21 MAY 1983, WEMBLEY STADIUM, Att. 100,000

Manchester United (1) **2** v **Brighton & Hove Albion** (1) **2**

Stapleton, Wilkins   Smith, Stevens

Manchester United: Bailey, Duxbury, Albiston, Wilkins, Moran, McQueen,

Robson, Muhren, Stapleton, Whiteside, Davies

FA CUP FINAL REPLAY

26 MAY 1983, WEMBLEY STADIUM, Att. 92,000

Manchester United (3) **4** v **Brighton & Hove Albion** (0) **0**

Robson (2), Whiteside,
Muhren (pen)

Manchester United: Bailey, Duxbury, Albiston, Wilkins, Moran, McQueen,

Robson, Muhren, Stapleton, Whiteside, Davies

FA Cup 1985

Everton, the FA Cup holders, were at Wembley attempting to win not only the League and Cup Double but also possibly a historic Treble of FA Cup, First Division Championship and European Cup Winners' Cup (indeed they had already won the latter two trophies). In 1977 United had ended Liverpool's hopes of the Double by defeating them in the FA Cup final, and on 18 May 1985 the Reds did the same thing to Liverpool's Merseyside neighbours. Although United won the game 1–0 thanks to a superb strike from Norman Whiteside, the game will be remembered more for Kevin Moran's sending-off. Moran became the first player to be dismissed in an FA Cup final when retired police inspector Peter Willis brandished the red card following a tackle on Peter Reid. Moran was inconsolable as his team-mates battled on without him. The game ended 0–0 after 90 minutes, but in the 110th minute Norman Whiteside curled a magnificent shot past Neville Southall in the Everton goal to give United the Cup.

FA CUP FINAL

18 MAY 1985, WEMBLEY STADIUM, Att. 100,000

Manchester United (1) **1**   v   **Everton** (0) **0** aet

Whiteside

Manchester United: Bailey, Gidman, Albiston (Duxbury),
Whiteside, McGrath, Moran, Robson, Strachan,
Hughes, Stapleton, Olsen

DID YOU KNOW THAT?
Moran was not awarded his winner's medal after the game and had to wait several days before the FA agreed that he should receive it.

FA Cup 1990

Crystal Palace took the lead in the 18th minute with a goal from Gary O'Reilly, only for Bryan Robson to pull United level in the 35th minute. Mark Hughes twisted and scored with a bullet-like shot from inside the area to put United 2–1 ahead after 62 minutes. Former Old Trafford hero Steve Coppell, the Crystal Palace manager, sent on Ian Wright, who scored within three minutes of taking the field to force extra time. Wright sent the Palace fans into a frenzy when he scored his second, and Palace's third, goal of the game two minutes into extra time. But there was still another twist to come, and in the 117th minute Mark Hughes drew the Reds level with another stunning goal. The match ended 3–3.

If the first game had been a thriller, then the second was the opposite. One goal settled in United's favour, Lee Martin just before the hour mark. This was Alex Ferguson's first trophy as United boss. Many more would follow...

FA CUP FINAL
12 MAY 1990, WEMBLEY STADIUM, Att. 80,000

Manchester United (1) **3**   v   **Crystal Palace** (1) **3**

Robson, Hughes (2)   O'Reilly, Wright (2)

Manchester United: Leighton, Ince, Martin (Blackmore), Bruce, Phelan, Pallister (Robins), Robson, Webb, McClair, Hughes, Wallace

FA CUP FINAL REPLAY
17 MAY 1990, WEMBLEY STADIUM, Att. 80,000

Manchester United (0) **1**   v   **Crystal Palace** (0) **0**

Martin

Manchester United: Sealey, Ince, Martin, Bruce, Phelan, Pallister, Robson, Webb, McClair, Hughes, Wallace

League Cup 1992

In April 1992, United were pushing for the First Division title and for success in the League Cup (then known as the Rumbelows League Cup), having exited the FA Cup in the fourth round. In this their third final in the competition, United overcame a strong Nottingham Forest side thanks to a 14th-minute goal from Brian McClair. The victory made up for the defeat to Sheffield Wednesday in the 1991 final. Although United first entered the League Cup competition in 1960–61, this was the first time the club had won it. On their way to lifting the trophy, United remained unbeaten in the competition, even though they played home and away legs in the second round.

LEAGUE CUP FINAL

12 APRIL 1992, WEMBLEY STADIUM, Att. 76,810

Manchester United (1) **1**   v   **Nottingham Forest** (0) **0**

McClair

Manchester United: Schmeichel, Parker, Irwin, Bruce, Phelan, Pallister, Kanchelskis (Sharpe), Ince, McClair, Hughes, Giggs)

Sub (not used): Webb

DID YOU KNOW THAT?

Two of the Nottingham Forest team would go on to earn numerous medals with United in the 1990s and beyond: Roy Keane and Teddy Sheringham. In addition, United's unused substitute Neil Webb was a former Forest player – and he would return there in November 1992.

DID YOU KNOW THAT?

This was the last major match in the famous career of Forest manager Brian Clough, who retired 13 months later.

FA Cup 1994

United, the Premier League champions, went into the 1994 FA Cup final knowing that a win would ensure their place in history, since they would become only the sixth team to win English football's coveted double. Chelsea had already defeated the Reds home and away in the League during the season and were looking to thwart them for a third time. They were partially successful because, on a rain-soaked Wembley pitch, the first-half ended goalless. But the day belonged to United and Eric Cantona, who scored with penalties after 60 and 66 minutes. A third goal, from Mark Hughes, three minutes after Cantona's second spot-kick, stretched the United advantage and a last-minute Brian McClair goal completed a thumping 4–0 win. It was United's eighth FA Cup success; more importantly it was the Reds' first ever double.

FA CUP FINAL
14 MAY 1994, WEMBLEY STADIUM, Att. 79,634

Manchester United (0) **4**   v   **Chelsea** (0) **0**

Cantona (2) (2 pens),
Hughes, McClair

Manchester United: Schmeichel, Parker, Irwin (Sharpe),
Bruce, Kanchelskis (McClair), Pallister, Cantona,
Ince, Keane, Hughes, Giggs
Sub (not used): Walsh.

DID YOU KNOW THAT?
Eric Cantona could have completed a rare FA Cup final hat-trick, but he passed to Brian McClair for him to knock the ball into the net for the fourth United goal.

FA Cup 1996

What most people remember about this final is the Liverpool players walking onto the Wembley pitch prior to the game in cream-coloured suits. The match itself was a rather drab affair, with both teams' flair players being stifled. The only goal of the final came in the 85th minute, when Eric Cantona rifled a punched clearance from David James into the net from the edge of the penalty area. United's 1–0 victory made them the first team in history to win English football's domestic double twice.

<u>FA CUP FINAL</u>

11 MAY 1996, WEMBLEY STADIUM, Att. 79,007

Manchester United (0) **1**   **v**   **Liverpool** (0) **0**

Cantona

Manchester United: Schmeichel, Irwin, P. Neville, May, Keane, Pallister, Cantona, Beckham (G. Neville), Cole (Scholes), Butt, Giggs)

Sub (not used): Sharpe.

DID YOU KNOW THAT?
Eric Cantona made his comeback, following the seven-month ban, against Liverpool and scored in the 2–2 draw at Old Trafford at the end of October 1995. Such was his form over the rest of the season, despite missing more than two months of the campaign, Cantona was voted Footballer of the Year by the Football Writers' Association.

DID YOU KNOW THAT?
United did not lose an FA Cup tie away from Wembley Stadium between February 1993, when they lost to Sheffield United and February 1997, when Wimbledon won a replay.

FA Cup 1999

Six days after recapturing their Premiership crown from Arsenal, United were at Wembley to face Newcastle United for the second leg of the historic Treble they were chasing in 1999. Despite Roy Keane suffering an early injury and having to leave the field after nine minutes, United ran out 2–0 winners with goals from Teddy Sheringham, after 11 minutes, and Paul Scholes, 13 minutes into the second half. It was United's tenth FA Cup victory.

FA CUP FINAL

22 MAY 1999, WEMBLEY STADIUM, Att. 79,101

Manchester United (1) **2**   **v**   **Newcastle United** (0) **0**

Sheringham, Scholes

Manchester United: Schmeichel, G. Neville, May, Johnsen, P. Neville, Beckham, Scholes (Stam), Keane (Sheringham), Giggs, Cole (Yorke), Solskjaer

Subs (not used): Van der Gouw, Blomqvist.

DID YOU KNOW THAT?
The introduction of Teddy Sheringham, in place of the injured Roy Keane was an inspired move by Alex Ferguson. The England striker scored less than two minutes after coming onto the pitch.

DID YOU KNOW THAT?
Only six teams completed the double of FA Cup and League championship in the 106 seasons 1888–1993 – Preston North End in 1889, Aston Villa in 1897, Tottenham Hotspur in 1961, Arsenal in 1971 and 1998 and Liverpool in 1986 – but this was United's third double in six seasons 1994–99.

FA Cup 2004

This game was one of the most one-sided FA Cup finals ever played. From the very first minute Millwall simply appeared to be only too happy to be in the final, safe in the knowledge that regardless of the result they would be playing European football at the Den the following season as United had already qualified for the UEFA Champions League. Ronaldo opened the scoring in the first half for United with van Nistelrooy adding a second just before half-time. In the second half United took their foot off the pedal but still managed to score a third goal when van Nistelrooy found the net a second time.

FA CUP FINAL

22 MAY 2004, MILLENNIUM STADIUM, CARDIFF, Att. 72,350

Manchester United (1) **3**   **v**   **Millwall** (0) **0**

Ronaldo,

Van Nistelrooy 2 (1 pen)

Manchester United: Howard (Carroll), G. Neville, O'Shea,

Brown, Silvestre, Ronaldo (Solskjaer), Fletcher (Butt),

van Nistelrooy, Scholes, Giggs

Subs (not used): P. Neville, Djemba-Djemba.

DID YOU KNOW THAT?

When Millwall's Curtis Weston replaced his player-manager Dennis Wise in the dying seconds of the match, he became the youngest player ever to appear in the FA Cup final. Aged 17 years and 119 days, Weston broke the record previously held by James Prinsep, who played for Clapham Rovers in 1879. The misery of defeat for Weston was tempered somewhat, because his favourite team as he grew up was Manchester United.

League Cup 2006

Manchester United met FA Premier League newcomers, Wigan Athletic, in the 2006 Carling Cup final. It was United's sixth appearance in the Final following defeats to Liverpool (1983), Sheffield Wednesday (1991), Aston Villa (1994) and Liverpool (2003) and their victory over Nottingham Forest in the 1992 Final. In contrast their Lancashire neighbours were making their first appearance in a major final. En route to the final United disposed of Barnet, West Bromwich Albion, Birmingham City and Blackburn Rovers. The final turned out to be one of the most one-sided since United defeated Chelsea in the FA Cup 4–0 at Wembley Stadium in 1994. This 4–0 win was the biggest margin of victory in the final in the history of the League Cup. Wayne Rooney opened the scoring after 33 minutes, but United settled the match with three goals in six minutes around the hour mark, Louis Saha, Cristiano Ronaldo and Rooney, again, being on target. Two-goal hero Rooney was named the Man of the Match.

LEAGUE CUP FINAL

26 FEBRUARY 2006, MILLENNIUM STADIUM, CARDIFF, Att. 66,866

Manchester United (1) **4**   **v**   **Wigan Athletic** (0) **0**

Rooney (2), Saha, Ronaldo

Manchester United: Van der Sar, G. Neville, Brown (Vidic),

Ferdinand, Silvestre (Evra), Ronaldo (Richardson),

O'Shea, Giggs, Park, Saha, Rooney.

Subs (not used): Howard, van Nistelrooy.

DID YOU KNOW THAT?

It was a nightmare match for Wigan's former United youth team keeper Mike Pollitt. He was carried off after 14 minutes.

League Cup 2009

Modern technology is a wonderful thing. Just ask United goal-keeper Ben Foster, who had studied film of penalties taken by Tottenham Hotspur players on his mobile phone. The 2009 Carling Cup final could not be called a classic and, after a 120 minutes of trying, neither team had managed to break the deadlock. That meant it was down to the dreaded penalty shoot-out and this is where Foster took over. Ryan Giggs took the first kick and made no mistake. Tottenham's first attempt came from Jamie O'Hara and Foster made a good save. The next three kicks, from Carlos Tevez, Vedran Corluka and Cristiano Ronaldo, all found the target, so United led 3–1. David Bentley took the third Spurs kick and he, like O'Hara before him, was denied by the England keeper. Up stepped Anderson, knowing a successful kick would win the Cup, and he made no mistake, shooting past his Brazilian compatriot Heurelho Gomes.

LEAGUE CUP FINAL

1 MARCH 2009, WEMBLEY STADIUM, Att. 88,217

Manchester United (0) **0** v **Tottenham Hotspur** (0) **0**

After extra time. Manchester United win 4–1 on penalties

Manchester United: Foster, O'Shea (Vidic), J. Evans, Ferdinand,

Evra, Ronaldo, Scholes, Gibson (Giggs),

Nani, Tévez, Welbeck (Anderson)

Sub; (not used): Kuszczak, Eckersley, Park , Rodrigo

DID YOU KNOW THAT?

This was the first of what United fans hoped would be a unique clean sweep of trophies. Unfortunately, Everton beat United on penalties in the FA Cup semi-final and Barcelona triumphed in the UEFA Champions League final.

League Cup 2010

United became only the third club to retain the Football League Cup as they came from behind to beat Aston Villa at Wembley Stadium. Sir Alex's men made a terrible start as Nemanja Vidic conceded a fifth-minute penalty for a foul on Gabriel Agbonlahor and was fortunate not to receive a card of any colour (especially as he got a yellow midway through the second half). James Milner converted the spotkick. But United replied seven minutes later, when Michael Owen fired home the equaliser, courtesy of a Richard Dunne slip. The Reds gradually took control of the match and Park Ji-sung hit a post just before half-time, soon after Owen had limped off with a hamstring injury, his match – and season – over. But there can be few more dangerous substitutes than Wayne Rooney. And it was Rooney who popped up with the match-winner, heading home a cross from man of the match Antonio Valencia. Rooney also hit an upright late on.

LEAGUE CUP FINAL

28 FEBRUARY 2010, WEMBLEY STADIUM, Att. 88,596

Manchester United (1) **2**   v   **Aston Villa** (1) **1**

Owen, Rooney   Milner (pen)

Manchester United: Kuszczak, Rafael (G. Neville), Vidic, J. Evans, Evra, Valencia, Fletcher, Carrick, Park, (Gibson), Owen (Rooney), Berbatov.

Subs (not used): Foster, Brown, Scholes, Biram Diouf

DID YOU KNOW THAT?

From the League Cup's first staging in 1960, the competition has had eight different sponsors, including the Milk Marketing Board, Coca-Cola and, most recently, Carabao.

FA Cup 2016

This game was a repeat of the 1990 FA Cup final, when Manchester United won a replay 1–0, thanks to a Lee Martin goal, after a 3–3 draw. Chris Smalling was sent off in the 70th minute and United went 1–0 down with just 12 minutes remaining. Until Palace scored, United had been on top – Anthony Martial and Marouane Fellaine both hitting the woodwork. However, a goal from Juan Mata in the 81st minute was enough to force extra time, and in the 110th minute Jesse Lingard won the game. This was United's 12th victory in the FA Cup. It also ended their 12-year wait for the FA Cup to return to the Old Trafford trophy cabinet.

FA CUP FINAL
21 MAY 2016, WEMBLEY STADIUM, ATT: 88,610

Manchester United (0) **2**   v   **Crystal Palace** (0) **1**

Mata, Lingard   Puncheon

Manchester United: De Gea, Valencia, Smalling, Blind,

Rojo (Darmian 66 mins), Carrick, Fellaini, Mata (Lingard 90 mins),

Rooney, Martial, Rashford (Young 72 mins)

Subs (not used): Romero, Jones, Schneiderlin, Herrera

DID YOU KNOW THAT?
Louis van Gaal became the third Dutch manager to win the FA Cup, after Ruud Gullit (Chelsea 1997) and Guus Hiddink (Chelsea 2009).

DID YOU KNOW THAT?
Manchester United have won both FA Cup Finals in which they had a player sent off (1985 and 2016).

League Cup 2017

Manchester United met Southampton in the 2017 EFL Cup Final at Wembley Stadium. In their second League Cup final the Saints were looking for their first win, while United were chasing a fifth triumph in nine attempts. Southampton began the game well but were trailing 2–0 after a sublime 25-yard Zlatan Ibrahimovic free-kick in the 19th minute and a well taken goal by Jesse Lingard in the 38th minute. Manolo Gabbiadini pulled a goal back on the stroke of half-time and, three minutes after the interval, the Saints drew level with Gabbiadini's second goal. The match looked destined for extra-time until Ibrahimovic powered in a header from an Ander Herrera cross with just three minutes remaining, his 26th goal in 38 games for United. He collected the Alan Hardaker Trophy after being named Man of the Match. It was United's second Wembley silverware of 2016–17 – the Reds had defeated Leicester City in the FA Community Shield – and sixth consecutive win at the stadium.

LEAGUE CUP FINAL

26 FEBRUARY 2017, WEMBLEY STADIUM, Att. 85,264

Manchester United (2) **3**   v   **Southampton** (1) **2**

Ibrahimovic (2), Lingard   Gabbiadini (2)

Manchester United: De Gea, Valencia, Bailly, Smalling, Rojo, Herrera, Pogba, Lingard (Rashford 77), Mata (Carrick 46), Martial (Fellaini 90), Ibrahimovic

DID YOU KNOW THAT?

Jesse Lingard has scored in his past three appearances for United at Wembley Stadium, netting in the 2016 FA Cup Final, 2016 FA Community Shield and 2017 League Cup Final.

The ones that got away

As well as their 12 FA Cup final victories and five successes in the League Cup, Manchester United have been beaten in seven FA Cup finals and four times in the League Cup. These were the days when things didn't go according to plan:

FA CUP FINAL

4 MAY 1957, WEMBLEY STADIUM
Aston Villa 2   v   **Manchester United 1**

3 MAY 1958, WEMBLEY STADIUM
Bolton Wanderers 2   v   **Manchester United 0**

1 MAY 1976, WEMBLEY STADIUM
Southampton 1   v   **Manchester United 0**

12 MAY 1979, WEMBLEY STADIUM
Arsenal 3   v   **Manchester United 2**

20 MAY 1995, WEMBLEY STADIUM
Everton 1   v   **Manchester United 0**

21 MAY 2005, MILLENNIUM STADIUM, CARDIFF
Arsenal 0   v   **Manchester United 0**
(Arsenal won 5-4 on penalties after extra-time)

19 MAY 2007, WEMBLEY STADIUM
Chelsea 1   v   **Manchester United 0**

LEAGUE CUP FINAL

26 MARCH 1983, WEMBLEY STADIUM
Liverpool 2   v   **Manchester United 1**

21 APRIL 1991, WEMBLEY STADIUM
Sheffield Wednesday 1   v   **Manchester United 0**

27 MARCH 1994, WEMBLEY STADIUM
Aston Villa 3   v   **Manchester United 1**

2 MARCH 2003, MILLENNIUM STADIUM, CARDIFF
Liverpool 2   v   **Manchester United 0**

TALK OF THE DEVILS

As the best supported team in England, and one of the world's most popular, literally millions of words have been spoken about Manchester United, both current and former players and staff as well as the media and opponents. At all clubs, the manager holds a regular weekly press conference and Jose Mourinho is no different. And players and coaches alike are asked for their comments after every match so, you can see, thousands of new snippets come to light every season.

On the following pages you will find 50 of the most insightful quotes made by a variety of people all on specific themes. Some are funny, some are sad, but all capture what it means to play for or against United. Each theme captures the essence of the Reds, such as Gary Neville's observations on his first visit to Old Trafford and on his brother Phil's departure from United to Everton.

Many of these quotes will be known to all United fans, such as Eric Cantona's enigmatic observations about seagulls following trawlers in March 1995, but hopefully others will be completely new, such as Ryan Giggs' modesty as he set United club records every time he set foot on the pitch. A quote without context is often just a stream of words; thus there are explanations for many of the pronouncements.

The Manchester United ethos

1

"For men who work on the shop floor, the one highlight of their week is to go and watch football. Matt Busby used to say 'you should give that man something he can't do himself, something exciting.' That's why Manchester United always play attacking football."

SIR BOBBY CHARLTON

2

"At the end of the game you're knackered and there are times when you come out of the shower when you feel you can hardly walk. But if I came off the pitch and didn't feel like that, I'd feel as if I'd cheated myself by not running my hardest."

WAYNE ROONEY

3

"You go to any factory or office and not everyone is going to like each other. Of course, you are going to have clashes. It's not to say we won't have a good do at Christmas and come Saturday, we will all want to win."

ROY KEANE

4

"This team never loses. They just run out of time."

STEVE McCLAREN, former United coach

5

"When you're in the tunnel and you hear: 'Please welcome the champions of England, the champions of Europe and the champions of the world,' you just believe that you're going to crush anybody in your way."

DIMITAR BERBATOV

George Best

1

"He treated my dad with a lot of respect and always took time out for him. I mean, little things are important to us and Matt even remembered what sort of sandwiches my dad liked."

GEORGE BEST, on Sir Matt Busby

2

"We had a few problems with the wee fella, but I prefer to remember his genius."

SIR MATT

3

"George Best has ice in his veins, warmth in his heart and timing and balance in his feet."

DANNY BLANCHFLOWER, George's last Northern Ireland manager

4

"Anyone that witnessed what George could do on the pitch wished they could do the same. He made an immense contribution to the game, and enriched the lives of everyone that saw him play. It is a very sad day."

SIR BOBBY CHARLTON, on learning of George's death in November 2005

5

"The closest I got to him was when we shook hands at the end of the game."

ROY FAIRFAX, the Northampton Town defender assigned to mark George when he netted six goals in United's 8–2 FA Cup win in 1970

Joining United

1

"I had always had a feeling that one day I would join United. I don't know whether it was wishful thinking or just a sixth sense about my destiny."

DENIS LAW

2

"I'm in love with Manchester United. It is like finding a wife who has given me the perfect marriage."

ERIC CANTONA

3

"Arriving at Old Trafford is moving to the highest level – there is nowhere else to go now."

MICHAEL CARRICK, arriving at Old Trafford in July 2006

4

"My dad tells me that I've always wanted to play here. He said when I first saw Old Trafford I just stood and stared for an hour."

GARY NEVILLE

5

"When I knew about the bid from United there was only one place I was going to go. The players here are unbelievable, the club has fans all over the world and hopefully I can do well."

WAYNE ROONEY

Ryan Giggs

1

"For a Welshman, I can't sing."

RYAN GIGGS

2

"It got to the point where I just thought, 'I'm going to take everyone on.' And when I got through I just hit it as hard as I could. David Seaman got a lot of stick, but it really was the only place I could have put it to beat him."

GIGGS, describing his FA Cup semi-final match-winner in 1999

3

"Ryan just put his head down, ran like he always does, didn't pass and got lucky."

NICKY BUTT is less charitable about that goal

4

"Eric Cantona is a great player, but he is not as good as Ryan Giggs."

PETER SWALES, City chairman when Giggs was in their youth set-up

5

"Ryan Giggs is the detonator, the man who can make Manchester United explode."

JEAN TIGANA, the former Fulham boss, and another Giggs fan

6

"Records are not important to me at this stage and I don't consciously think about them, but they are something I will be able to look back on proudly when I have finished."

GIGGS

European nights

1

"Winning the European Cup in 1968 was a big thank you to the players that weren't with us, and even those of us who did survive. That night was something special. Everyone in the world wanted us to win at Wembley and doing so was part of the history – it was important the club managed it."

SIR BOBBY CHARLTON, reflecting in March 2008, on 1968

2

"For me, personally, I've had three European finals when it tipped down with rain, so when the rain came in Moscow I said, 'This will do for me; this will do.' I was delighted to see it and with [John] Terry slipping ... you know, it's amazing. Luck's luck, and you can't win without it."

SIR ALEX FERGUSON, after the 2008 Champions League final

3

"I couldn't tell you which hotel we stayed at, whether we had a post-match banquet ... it's just a blank. But the game itself, I can remember almost every kick. I was fortunate enough to score in the Final. I remember the ball being cleared and coming to me. And I knew I was going to score, I just knew."

GOERGE BEST, looking back at the 1968 European Cup final.

4

"It was an unbelievable night. I watched football as a kid and saw players go up to the Royal Box at Wembley and thought, 'What are they crying for?' But as soon as the final whistle went, I just sunk to my knees. I couldn't stop myself.'"

RYAN GIGGS, on that memorable night in 1999

United legends

1

"Sir Matt Busby came into the dressing room after we'd
become champions. He said very little but his expression said
it all. His beloved Manchester United were back on top."
BRYAN ROBSON, when United won their first championship for 26
years in 1993

2

"If he's got a temperament, wait until he sees my temperament."
ALEX FERGUSON, November 1992, when he signed Eric Cantona

3

"Over the years people called several players the new Duncan
Edwards ... first Dave Mackay, then Bryan Robson. But none of
them came close. He was the only player who ever made me
feel inferior."
SIR BOBBY CHARLTON on his Busby Babe team-mate Edwards

4

"Everybody now talks about Cantona being the main
catalyst of United's glories. But without Bryan Robson,
I maintain United might not have had the same stature
when Eric arrived. Robson was the essence of United."
RON ATKINSON, who managed Robson at West Brom and United

5

"When the seagulls follow the trawler, it is because they think
sardines will be thrown into the sea. Merci."
ERIC CANTONA's enigmatic utterance after his court case
in March 1995

Fond farewells

1

"Maybe I could come back, but only as number one."

ERIC CANTONA, August 2006

2

"I found it very difficult returning to Old Trafford for the first time. I got a marvellous reception, but the game just passed me by. Some of the Chelsea lads had a go at me after we scored. They reckoned I didn't jump up and down enough."

MARK HUGHES

3

"I feel really sad about leaving but I have to move on. I've always been a United fan and will always follow the team."

DAVID BECKHAM

4

"It has been a great honour and privilege for me to play for Manchester United for over 12 years... in front of the best supporters in the world."

ROY KEANE.

5

"After Philip left, I had half an hour to myself driving in my car and I did think: 'This isn't going to last forever. I'd better enjoy this."

GARY NEVILLE, after his brother Phil joined Everton in the summer of 2005

The lighter side

1

"Apparently when you head a football, you lose brain cells, but it doesn't bother me ... I'm a horse. No one's proved it yet, have they?"

DAVID MAY, United central defender, who headed a lot of balls

2

"I've sung every song in the world in the bath. I'm thinking of releasing a CD called *Singalong with Fergie*!"

SIR ALEX FERGUSON on a hidden talent

3

"It wasn't my choice to become a goalkeeper, but I was probably too violent to play outfield."

PETER SCHMEICHEL.

4

"The lads used to call me 'The Judge' because I sat on the bench so much."

LES SEALEY, former (mainly substitute) United goalkeeper

5

"We all agree, Jaap Stam is harder than Arnie!"

UNITED FANS serenade Jaap Stam during a December 2000 Champions League tie at the Schwarzenegger Stadium in Graz, Austria

Playing against United

1

"When you look down the list of who you are going to get points off, you mark Manchester United down as zero."
JIM SMITH, former Derby County manager

2

"I don't look at Manchester United. They've got 70,000 gates, they've got the Beckhams and so on, all young and hungry. My dream is to become second best – only then will I start worrying about the freaks from across the Pennines."
DAVID O'LEARY, when he was Leeds United manager

3

"I want our fans to be happy and for them to enjoy the experience of being at Old Trafford. I would appeal to them to just enjoy the performance we intend to put on for them."
FRANCSCO TOTTI, AS Roma captain, 2007, before United won 7–1

4

"In Turin, [Claudio] Gentile was marking me and I remember trying to get a cross in and he just stood on my shin. Later on, I was waiting for a corner and Gentile pulled a hair from under my armpit. I'd never had that before."
STEVE COPPELL recalls a tough night against Juventus in 1978

5

"I've got more respect for Ferguson than anyone else in the game. He is the master. He's like a Scouser, really. He's funny, and he even votes Labour. I love him."
JAMIE CARRAGHER

Sir Alex Ferguson

1

"The afternoon of 2 May 1993, when we were crowned the champions of England was the day I truly became the manager of Manchester United. Until that fancy bit of silverware was in our grasp, nothing could be taken for granted."

SIR ALEX FERGUSON reminisces

2

"Some of the players call me 'Gaffer' … and when Gary Pallister wants to take a weekend off, he calls me 'God'!."

SIR ALEX

3

"My wife's always saying, 'Why don't you grow up?' and I say, 'Why should I? I'm enjoying myself being silly and young!'"

SIR ALEX

4

"For the first year I was a pro, when the manager walked into the room I just shut up and sat up as if I was at school. If I heard him coming down the stairs, I would turn around and go back into the dressing room. I was definitely scared of him."

PHIL NEVILLE

5

"Football, eh! Bloody hell!."

SIR ALEX FERGUSON, just after United's stunning fight-back to win the 1999 UEFA Champions League final

CHAPTER

7

EUROPEAN
GLORY NIGHTS

Manchester United broke the mould for English football clubs in Europe. The Reds were the first English team to play in a European competition (the 1956–57 European Cup) the first English team to win the European Cup (1967–68), the only English team to appear in four UEFA Champions League finals (losing in 2009 and 2011) and the only English team to win the European Cup, Champions League and European Cup winners' Cup and the UEFA Europa League.

This impressive list doesn't take into account United's successes in the UEFA Super Cup and the FIFA World Club Cup and World Club Championships, all of which have been won. We could have filled this book with reports on other great nights, such as the one when AS Roma were dismantled 7–1, or the night in 1968, when the Reds clinched their first European Cup final berth.

Nevertheless, over the next few pages, you will be able to relive the glorious nights when Manchester United won the major European competitions. In addition to a brief report, you will find full match details, including the line-ups, goalscorers and all the substitutes. How good does this sound, "Manchester United, champions of the world, champions of Europe and champions of England?"

European Cup 1968

Many United followers consider this to be the greatest night in the history of the world's most famous football club. Ten years after the Munich Air Disaster, Matt Busby saw his dream fulfilled when his United team were crowned kings of Europe. A Wembley crowd of 100,000 watched United beat the champions of Portugal, Benfica, 4–1 after extra time. Bobby Charlton had given United the lead but Jaime Graca equalised. Just before the final whistle, Alex Stepney made a brilliant save to deny Eusebio what would been the winner. Inside less than ten minutes of the first period of extra-time, United made sure of the trophy as George Best, Brian Kidd – on his 19th birthday – and Charlton, again, scored. Benfica were broken and United could have scored more goals. Bobby Charlton, recalling those events of ten years earlier, couldn't hold back the tears as he collected the trophy.

EUROPEAN CUP FINAL

29 MAY 1968, WEMBLEY STADIUM, Att. 100,000

Manchester United (0) **4**   v   **Benfica** (0) **1** aet

Charlton (2), Best, Kidd   Graca

Manchester United: Stepney, Brennan, Dunne,

Crerand, Foulkes, Stiles, Best, Kidd,

Charlton, Sadler, Aston

DID YOU KNOW THAT?

Although the European Cup had started in 1955, United, the 1956 League champions, were the first English club to play in the competition. The Football League had banned Chelsea from participating in 1955, fearing fixture congestion.

European Cup Winners' Cup 1991

On their way to their 2–1 victory over the mighty Barcelona in the final of the 1991 European Cup Winners' Cup, United won all four of their away leg matches. They beat Pecsi Munkas 1–0, Wrexham 2–0, Montpellier 2–0 and Legia Warsaw 3–1. Mark Hughes, playing against the side that considered him a flop, scored both United goals in the final. With this success, United became the first English club to have won both the European Cup and the European Cup Winners' Cup. There was little to choose between the teams at Feyenoord's stadium in Rotterdam, until Hughes opened the scoring midway through the second half. Forced to chase the game, Barcelona left gaps in their defence and Hughes grabbed his second goal after 74 minutes. Five minutes later, Dutchman Ronald Koeman reduced the arrears, but United were able to play out time for a famous victory.

EUROPEAN CUP WINNERS' CUP FINAL
15 MAY 1991, FEYENOORD STADION, Att. 45,000

Manchester United (0) **2**   **v**   **Barcelona** (0) **1**

Hughes (2)   Koeman

Manchester United: Sealey, Irwin, Blackmore, Bruce,
Phelan, Pallister, Robson, Ince, McClair,
Hughes, Sharpe

DID YOU KNOW THAT?
United are uniquely placed to be the only English club to have won every major competition open to them. As previous winners of the European Cup Winners' Cup, they continued that trend by winning the Europa League (established 2009) in 2017.

UEFA Super Cup 1991

The 1991 European Super Cup was the 16th edition of the UEFA Super Cup and was contested by the winners of the European Cup and the European Cup Winners' Cup. The 1991 final saw Manchester United, holders of the European Cup Winners' Cup after beating FC Barcelona 2–1 in the final, play Red Star Belgrade who had defeated Olympique de Marseilles 5–3 on penalties (0–0 after extra-time) in the 1991 European Cup final. The 1991 UEFA Super Cup final was due to be played over two legs but as a result of the political unrest in Yugoslavia at the time, UEFA decided only one tie would be played and Old Trafford would host it. Red Star Belgrade's star player was Darko Pancev who won the 1991 European Golden Boot after scoring 34 goals for the Yugoslavian outfit. The game was settled in the 67th minute when Brian "Choccy" McClair scored the only goal of the game.

UEFA SUPER CUP FINAL
19 NOVEMBER 1991, OLD TRAFFORD, MANCHESTER Att: 22, 110

Manchester United (0) **1**   v   **Red Star Belgrade** (1) **0**

McLair

Manchester United: Schmeichel, Martin (Giggs 71), Irwin, Bruce (c), Webb, Pallister, Kanchelskis, Ince, McClair, Hughes, Blackmore

DID YOU KNOW THAT?
Since 2000, the UEFA Super Cup final has been contested by the winners of the UEFA Champions League and the winners of the UEFA Cup/UEFA Europa League.

UEFA Champions League 1999

On a balmy Spanish night Manchester United met Bayern Munich in the UEFA Champions League final at Barcelona's famous Nou Camp Stadium. Only five days earlier United had beaten Newcastle United in the FA Cup final at Wembley to clinch their third domestic Double. Now all that stood between United and a historic Treble was the German Champions, Bayern Munich, who ironically had been in the same group as United in the early stages of the competition. Indeed, Bayern were chasing the second leg of their own Treble having already won the Bundesliga and being due to face Kaiserslautern in the German Cup final. Despite conceding an early goal to a Mario Basler free-kick and surviving numerous close calls during the course of the game, United won the Cup in dramatic fashion with late injury-time goals from Teddy Sheringham and Ole Gunnar Solskjaer.

UEFA CHAMPIONS LEAGUE FINAL
26 MAY 1999, NOU CAMP STADIUM, BARCELONA, Att. 90,000

Manchester United (0) **2**   v   **Bayern Munich** (1) **1**

Sheringham, Solskjaer   Basler

Manchester United: Schmeichel, G. Neville, Irwin, Johnsen,
Stam, Blomqvist (Sheringham), Butt, Giggs,
Beckham, Cole (Solskjaer), Yorke

DID YOU KNOW THAT?
After he scored the winning goal in Barcelona, Ole Gunnar Solskjaer did a celebratory slide on his knees. Unfortunately, in doing so, he damaged his ligaments and, by his own admission, was never the same player again.

UEFA Champions League 2008

The 2008 UEFA Champions League Final, in rainy Moscow, was the first all-English contest for Europe's biggest prize. On a night of high tension, it was Manchester United who came out on top beating Chelsea 6–5 on penalties after the teams had been level at 1–1 after 45, 90 and 120 minutes. The Reds had the better of the first half, and took the lead after 26 minutes when Cristiano Ronaldo headed home his 42nd goal of the season. Frank Lampard equalised for Chelsea just before half-time and the Blues were on top after the break, with both Lampard and Didier Drogba hitting the woodwork. The drama continued in extra-time and it exploded when Drogba was sent off for striking Nemanja Vidic. United couldn't take advantage of their extra player, so it went to penalties. Petr Cech saved Ronaldo's attempt, United's first, and Chelsea would have won the Cup if skipper John Terry had not slipped and missed his effort. It went to sudden death and after Ryan Giggs – on his record-setting 759th United appearance – had converted his try, Edwin van der Sar saved from Nicolas Anelka to give United their third European Cup.

UEFA CHAMPIONS LEAGUE FINAL

22 MAY 2008, LUZHNIKI STADIUM, MOSCOW, Att. 69,552

Manchester United (1) **1**   **v**   **Chelsea** (1) **1**

Cristiano Ronaldo   Lampard

United won 6–5 on penalties after extra time

Manchester United: Van der Sar, Brown (Anderson), Ferdinand,
Vidic, Evra, Hargreaves, Scholes (Giggs), Carrick,
Ronaldo, Tevez, Rooney (Nani)

Subs: Kuszczak, O'Shea, Fletcher, Silvestre

UEFA Europa League 2017

Manchester United claimed their third trophy of the season and a first ever UEFA Europa League triumph, beating Ajax 2–0, thanks to goals from Paul Pogba and Henrikh Mkhitaryan in the Friends Arena, Stockholm, Sweden. The Reds became the first British club to win all three major European trophies – a task more difficult to achieve since the end of the European Cup-winners' Cup in 1998. Pogba opened the scoring in the 18th minute and pointed to the sky having lost his father ten days earlier. Mkhitaryan's overhead kick in the 48th minute was historic because it was the Armenian's fifth away European goal for United, the most by any Manchester United player in a single season. It was the 45th time during the season that United scored first and went on to avoid defeat – 37 wins and eight draws. The win was Jose Mourinho's seventh win over the Dutch side in his seven meetings against them as a manager and he became the first coach to win the European Cup/UEFA Champions League (FC Porto 2004, Inter Milan 2010) and UEFA Cup/UEFA Europa League (Porto 2003, Manchester United 2017) with different teams. It also maintained his 100 per cent record of winning every major European Cup final as a manager.

UEFA EUROPA LEAGUE FINAL

24 MAY 2017, FRIENDS ARENA, STOCKHOLM Att: 46,961

Manchester United (1) 2   v   **Ajax Amsterdam (0) 0**

Pogba, Mkhitaryan

Manchester United: Romero; Valencia (c), Smalling, Blind, Darmian; Herrera, Fellaini, Mkhitaryan (Lingard 74), Pogba, Mata (Rooney 90), Rashford (Martial 84)

Subs not used: De Gea, Fosu-Mensah, Jones, Carrick.

CHAPTER 8

SING YOUR HEARTS OUT FOR THE LADS

Manchester United's fans are considered to be some of the most fanatical in the world and they help to make the atmosphere at Old Trafford the cauldron of sound that it is. There are few experiences than can match the sound of a full house of 76,000 United fans cheering and singing for the mighty Reds.

The repertoire of songs chanted by the United faithful is varied, some paying homage to the team and some specifically about the Old Trafford stars. Of course, when one of the Reds heroes moves on to pastures new, a different chant must be found for his replacement, so song-leaders must be able to think quickly and musically.

Over the next few pages you will find a number of songs, from classics like 'Que Sera, Sera...' and 'Glory, Glory Man United', to player-specific anthems lauding the talents of Old Trafford legends like Wayne Rooney and Ryan Giggs.

Of course, when you go to Old Trafford, you will hear many other songs, not only honouring the United players but also those – and they are rather less flattering – against the opposition. So, clear your throat, take a deep breath and sing ...

The Flowers Of Manchester

One cold and bitter Thursday in Munich Germany,
Eight great football stalwarts conceded victory,
Eight men will never play again who met destruction there,
The Flowers of British football, the Flowers of Manchester.

Matt Busby's boys were flying, returning from Belgrade,
This great United family, all masters of their trade,
The pilot of the aircraft, the skipper Captain Thain,
Three times they tried to take off and twice turned back again.

The third time down the runway disaster followed close,
There was slush upon that runway and the aircraft never rose,
It ploughed into the marshy ground, it broke, it overturned
And eight of the team were killed when the blazing wreckage burned.

Roger Byrne & Tommy Taylor who were capped for England's side
And Ireland's Billy Whelan and England's Geoff Bent died,
Mark Jones and Eddie Colman, and David Pegg also,
They lost their lives as it ploughed on through the snow.

Big Duncan he went too, with an injury to his frame,
And Ireland's brave Jack Blanchflower will never play again,
The great Matt Busby lay there, the father of his team,
Three long months passed by before he saw his team again.

The trainer, coach and secretary, and a member of the crew,
Also eight sporting journalists who with United flew,
And one of them Big Swifty, who we will ne'er forget,
The finest English 'keeper that ever graced the net.
Oh, England's finest football team its record truly great,
Its proud successes mocked by a cruel turn of fate.
Eight men will never play again, who met destruction there,
The Flowers of English football, the Flowers of Manchester.

The Red Flag

United's flag is deepest red
It shrouded all our Munich dead
Before their limbs grew stiff and cold
Their heart's blood dyed it's ev'ry fold
Then raise United's banner high
Beneath it's shade we'll live and die
So keep the faith and never fear
We'll keep the Red Flag flying here
We'll never die, we'll never die
We'll never die, we'll never die
We'll keep the Red flag flying high
'Cos Man United will never die

The United Calypso

Manchester, Manchester United;
A bunch of bouncing Busby Babes;
They deserve to be knighted!
If ever they are playing in your town;
You must get to that football ground;
Take a lesson come and see;
Football taught by Matt Busby.

Que sera, sera

Que sera, sera.
Whatever will be. will be,
We're going to Wembley,
Que sera, sera.

Glory Glory Man United

Glory, glory, Man United,
Glory, glory, Man United,
Glory, glory, Man United,
And the Reds go marching on, on, on.
Just like the Busby Babes in Days gone by
We'll keep the Red Flags flying high
You've got to see yourself from far and wide
You've got to hear the masses sing with pride
United! Man United!
Glory Glory Man United
Glory Glory Man United
Glory Glory Man United
As the Reds Go Marching On! On! On! (3x)

United Road Take Me Home

Take me home,
United Road,.
To a place that I belong,
To Old Trafford,
To see United,
Take me home,
United Road.

To the tune of *Country Roads* by John Denver

He Scores Goals

He scores goals, galore,
He scores goals!
He scores goals, galore,
He scores goals!
He scores goals, galore,
He scores goals!
Paul Scholes - he scores goals...

To the tune of *Kum Ba Yah*

Running down the Wing

Ryan Giggs, Ryan Giggs, running down the wing,
Ryan Giggs, Ryan Giggs, running down the wing -
Loved by the reds, feared by the blues...
Ryan Giggs, Ryan Giggs, Ryan Giggs.

To the tune of *Robin Hood*

The White Pele

I saw my mate the other day,
He said to me, he'd seen the white Pele,
So I asked, "Who is he?"
He goes by the name of Wayne Rooney.
Wayne Rooney, Wayne Rooney,
Goes by the name of Wayne Rooney.

CHAPTER

9

THE UPS AND DOWNS
OF UNITED

The most feared word in the Premier League lexicon is the "R" word: relegation, that moment when your club's membership of England's elite competition comes to an end and the financial benefits of playing in the top flight disappear.

For United, it is more than 40 years since the unthinkable became realilty and the Reds went down. In those days it was from Division One to Division Two; now, of course, it is from the Premiership to the Championship. The mark of the greatest teams is that these spells in the lower divisions are very brief and for United, since World War 2, there has just been one season when they were not in the top flight.

This section features the seasons which saw United lose their First Division status on one page and how they regained their place at the top table on the next. Each season is reviewed and the full league table shows how close United were to avoiding the dreaded drop or by how much they bounced back.

For United, and with most clubs, relegation is the chance to clean house, to sweep away the problems that caused relegation and to start afresh, often with bright young talent. Most United fans are too young to remember the despair of facing the drop – or even a relegation struggle for that matter – but no team has a divine right to play at the highest level.

Going Down 1893–94

After only two seasons in the First Division, Newton Heath was relegated in season 1893–94 after losing their Test Match 2–0 against Liverpool, played at Blackburn on 28 April 1894. The Heathens avoided relegation at the end of their first season in the top flight by beating Small Heath 6–3 on aggregate over two Test Matches.

DID YOU KNOW THAT?

The Test Match system which decided promotion and relegation in the early years of the Football League meant that teams at the bottom of Division 1 played those at the top of Division 2, with the winners going into the top level.

Football League Division 1 **1893–94**

		P	W	D	L	F	A	W	D	L	F	A	Pts
1.	Aston Villa	30	12	2	1	49	13	7	4	4	35	29	44
2.	Sunderland	30	11	3	1	46	14	6	1	8	26	30	38
3.	Derby County	30	9	2	4	47	32	7	2	6	26	30	36
4.	Blackburn Rovers	30	13	0	2	48	15	3	2	10	21	38	34
5.	Burnley	30	13	0	2	43	17	2	4	9	18	34	34
6.	Everton	30	11	1	3	63	23	4	2	9	27	34	33
7.	Nottingham Forest	30	10	2	3	38	16	4	2	9	19	32	32
8.	WBA	30	8	4	3	35	23	6	0	9	31	36	32
9.	Wolverhampton W	30	11	1	3	34	24	3	2	10	18	39	31
10.	Sheffield United	30	8	3	4	26	22	5	2	8	21	39	31
11.	Stoke City	30	13	1	1	45	17	0	2	13	20	62	29
12.	Sheffield Wednesday	30	7	3	5	32	21	2	5	8	16	36	26
13.	Bolton Wanderers	30	7	3	5	18	14	3	1	11	20	38	24
14.	Preston North End	30	7	1	7	25	24	3	2	10	19	32	23
15.	Darwen	30	6	4	5	25	28	1	1	13	12	55	19
16.	**Newton Heath**	**30**	**5**	**2**	**8**	**29**	**33**	**1**	**0**	**14**	**7**	**39**	**14**

Test match: Liverpool 3, Newton Heath 0

Going Up 1905–06

The longest spell the club spent outside the top division was the 12 years between the first relegation and the promotion in 1906, their fourth season as Manchester United. In the two years before they finally went back up, United had finished third in the table missing out on promotion by one point in 1904 and by three a year later. They made no mistake in 1906, finishing nine points clear of third-placed Chelsea.

DID YOU KNOW THAT?
The two teams promoted from Division 2 in 1906 contested the 1909 FA Cup final, with United beating Bristol City 1–0.

Football League Division 2 **1905–06**

		P	W	D	L	F	A	W	D	L	F	A	Pts
1.	Bristol City	38	17	1	1	43	8	13	5	1	40	20	66
2.	**Manchester United**	**38**	**15**	**3**	**1**	**55**	**13**	**13**	**3**	**3**	**35**	**15**	**62**
3.	Chelsea	38	13	4	2	58	16	9	5	5	32	21	53
4.	WBA	38	13	4	2	53	16	9	4	6	26	20	52
5.	Hull City	38	10	5	4	38	21	9	1	9	29	33	44
6.	Leeds City	38	11	5	3	38	19	6	4	9	21	28	43
7.	Leicester City	38	10	3	6	30	21	5	9	5	23	27	42
8.	Grimsby Town	38	11	7	1	33	13	4	3	12	13	33	40
9.	Burnley	38	9	4	6	26	23	6	4	9	16	30	38
10.	Stockport County	38	11	6	2	36	16	2	3	14	8	40	35
11.	Bradford City	38	7	4	8	21	22	6	4	9	25	38	34
12.	Barnsley	38	11	4	4	45	17	1	5	13	15	45	33
13.	Lincoln City	38	10	1	8	46	29	2	5	12	23	43	30
14.	Blackpool	38	8	3	8	22	21	2	6	11	15	41	29
15.	Gainsborough Trinity	38	10	2	7	35	22	2	2	15	9	35	28
16.	Glossop North End	38	9	4	6	36	28	1	4	14	13	43	28
17.	Port Vale	38	10	4	5	34	25	2	0	17	15	57	28
18.	Chesterfield	38	8	4	7	26	24	4	13	14	14	48	28
19.	Burton United	38	9	4	6	26	20	1	2	16	8	47	26
20.	Leyton Orient	38	6	4	9	19	22	1	3	15	16	56	21

Going Down 1921–22

The inter-war years were not very good for Manchester United, with the club suffering three relegations in the 20 years 1919–39. The first drop came at the end of the 1921–22 season, when United finished bottom of the table, with eight wins and a meagre 28 points from their 42 League games, and eight points away from safety. During the season John Robson resigned as manager and he was replaced by John Chapman.

Football League Division 1 **1921–22**

		P	W	D	L	F	A	W	D	L	F	A	Pts
1.	Liverpool	42	15	4	2	43	15	7	9	5	20	21	57
2.	Tottenham Hotspur	42	15	3	3	43	17	6	6	9	22	22	51
3.	Burnley	42	16	3	2	49	18	6	2	13	23	36	49
4.	Cardiff City	42	13	2	6	40	26	6	8	7	21	27	48
5.	Aston Villa	42	16	3	2	50	19	6	0	15	24	36	47
6.	Bolton Wanderers	42	12	4	5	40	24	8	3	10	28	35	47
7.	Newcastle United	42	11	5	5	36	19	7	5	9	23	26	46
8.	Middlesbrough	42	12	6	3	46	19	4	8	9	33	50	46
9.	Chelsea	42	9	6	6	17	16	8	6	7	23	27	46
10.	Manchester City	42	13	7	1	44	21	5	2	14	21	49	45
11.	Sheffield United	42	11	3	7	32	17	4	7	10	27	37	40
12.	Sunderland	42	13	4	4	46	23	3	4	14	14	39	40
13.	WBA	42	8	6	7	26	23	7	4	10	25	40	40
14.	Huddersfield Town	42	12	3	6	33	14	3	6	12	20	40	39
15.	Blackburn Rovers	42	7	6	8	35	31	6	6	9	19	26	38
16.	Preston North End	42	12	7	2	33	20	1	5	15	9	45	38
17.	Arsenal	42	10	6	5	27	19	5	1	15	20	37	37
18.	Birmingham City	42	9	2	10	25	29	6	5	10	23	31	37
19.	Oldham Athletic	42	8	7	6	21	15	5	4	12	17	35	37
20.	Everton	42	10	7	4	42	22	2	5	14	15	33	36
21.	Bradford City	42	8	5	8	28	30	3	5	13	20	42	32
22.	**Manchester United**	**42**	**7**	**7**	**7**	**25**	**26**	**1**	**5**	**15**	**16**	**47**	**28**

Going Up 1924–25

After three seasons in Division Two United were promoted back into Division One. On their way to securing promotion United finished runners-up in the League conceding just 23 goals from their 42 League games. This was a record for Division Two.

DID YOU KNOW THAT?
United had been three points away from promotion in 1923.

Football League Division 2 **1924–25**

		P	W	D	L	F	A	W	D	L	F	A	Pts
1.	Leicester City	42	15	4	2	58	9	9	7	5	32	23	59
2.	**Manchester United**	**42**	**17**	**3**	**1**	**40**	**6**	**6**	**8**	**7**	**17**	**17**	**57**
3.	Derby County	42	15	3	3	49	15	7	8	6	22	21	55
4.	Portsmouth	42	7	13	1	28	14	8	5	8	30	36	48
5.	Chelsea	42	11	8	2	31	12	5	7	9	20	25	47
6.	Wolverhampton W	42	14	1	6	29	19	6	5	10	26	32	46
7.	Southampton	42	12	8	1	29	10	1	10	10	11	26	44
8.	Port Vale	42	12	4	5	34	19	5	4	12	14	37	42
9.	Gateshead	42	9	6	6	33	21	3	11	7	9	17	41
10.	Hull City	42	12	6	3	40	14	3	5	13	10	35	41
11.	Leyton Orient	42	8	7	6	22	13	6	5	10	20	29	40
12.	Fulham	42	11	6	4	26	15	4	4	13	15	41	40
13.	Middlesbrough	42	6	10	5	22	21	4	9	8	14	23	39
14.	Sheffield Wednesday	42	12	3	6	36	23	3	5	13	14	33	38
15.	Barnsley	42	8	8	5	30	23	5	4	12	16	36	38
16.	Bradford City	42	11	6	4	26	13	2	6	13	11	37	38
17.	Blackpool	42	8	5	8	37	26	6	4	11	28	35	37
18.	Oldham Athletic	42	9	5	7	24	21	4	6	11	11	30	37
19.	Stockport County	42	10	6	5	26	15	3	5	13	11	42	37
20.	Stoke City	42	7	8	6	22	17	5	3	13	12	29	35
21.	Crystal Palace	42	8	4	9	23	19	4	6	11	15	35	34
22.	Coventry City	42	10	6	5	32	26	1	3	17	13	58	31

Going Down 1930–31

A 4–4 draw with Middlesbrough (Tom Reid 2, Ray Bennion, Stan Gallimore) was United's final League game of the 1930–31 season. United finished bottom of Division One, with 27 defeats from their 42 matches; it was their worst ever season for League defeats. Nine of the losses were at Old Trafford, which is also a club record figure. The team also suffered their worst ever season for away defeats, losing 18 of their 21 games. After the Middlesbrough game, Herbert Bamlett resigned as manager and Walter Crickmer took over.

Football League Division 1 **1930–31**

		P	W	D	L	F	A	W	D	L	F	A	Pts
1.	Arsenal	42	14	5	2	67	27	14	5	2	60	32	66
2.	Aston Villa	42	17	3	1	86	34	8	6	7	42	44	59
3.	Sheffield Wednesday	42	14	3	4	65	32	8	5	8	37	43	52
4.	Portsmouth	42	11	7	3	46	26	7	6	8	38	41	49
5.	Huddersfield Town	42	10	8	3	45	27	8	4	9	36	38	48
6.	Derby County	42	12	6	3	56	31	6	4	11	38	48	46
7.	Middlesbrough	42	13	5	3	57	28	6	3	12	41	62	46
8.	Manchester City	42	13	2	6	41	29	5	8	8	34	41	46
9.	Liverpool	42	11	6	4	48	28	4	6	11	38	57	42
10.	Blackburn Rovers	42	14	3	4	54	28	3	5	13	29	56	42
11.	Sunderland	42	12	4	5	61	38	4	5	12	28	47	41
12.	Chelsea	42	13	4	4	42	19	2	6	13	22	48	40
13.	Grimsby Town	42	13	2	6	55	31	4	3	14	27	56	39
14.	Bolton Wanderers	42	12	6	3	45	26	3	3	15	23	55	39
15.	Sheffield United	42	10	7	4	49	31	4	3	14	29	53	38
16.	Leicester City	42	12	4	5	50	38	4	2	15	30	57	38
17.	Newcastle United	42	9	2	10	41	45	6	4	11	37	42	36
18.	West Ham United	42	11	3	7	56	44	3	5	13	23	50	36
19.	Birmingham City	42	11	3	7	37	28	2	7	12	18	42	36
20.	Blackpool	42	8	7	6	41	44	3	3	15	30	81	32
21.	Leeds United	42	10	3	8	49	31	2	4	15	19	50	31
22.	**Manchester United**	**42**	**6**	**6**	**9**	**30**	**37**	**1**	**2**	**18**	**23**	**78**	**22**

Going Up 1935–36

With a 3–2 away win at Bury (Tom Manley 2, George Mutch) on 29 April 1936, United clinched the Second Division title, a point clear of Charlton Athletic. It was a far cry from two seasons earlier, when United almost suffered the ignominy of relegation down to Division Three North. Only one point separated United from relegated Millwall in 1934.

DID YOU KNOW THAT?
This was the first time United had topped Division 2.

Football League Division 2 **1935–36**

		P	W	D	L	F	A	W	D	L	F	A	Pts
1.	**Manchester United**	**42**	**16**	**3**	**2**	**55**	**16**	**6**	**9**	**6**	**30**	**27**	**56**
2.	Charlton Athletic	42	15	6	0	53	17	7	5	9	32	41	55
3.	Sheffield United	42	15	4	2	51	15	5	8	8	28	35	52
4.	West Ham United	42	13	5	3	51	23	9	3	9	39	45	52
5.	Tottenham Hotspur	42	12	6	3	60	25	6	7	8	31	30	49
6.	Leicester City	42	14	5	2	53	19	5	5	11	26	38	48
7.	Plymouth Argyle	42	15	2	4	50	20	5	6	10	21	37	48
8.	Newcastle United	42	13	5	3	56	27	7	1	13	32	52	46
9.	Fulham	42	11	6	4	58	24	4	8	9	18	28	44
10.	Blackpool	42	14	3	4	64	34	4	4	13	29	38	43
11.	Norwich City	42	14	2	5	47	24	3	7	11	25	41	43
12.	Bradford City	42	12	7	2	32	18	3	6	12	23	47	43
13.	Swansea City	42	11	3	7	42	26	4	6	11	25	50	39
14.	Bury	42	10	6	5	41	27	3	6	12	25	57	38
15.	Burnley	42	9	8	4	35	21	3	5	13	15	38	37
16.	Bradford Park Av	42	13	6	2	43	26	1	3	17	19	58	37
17.	Southampton	42	11	3	7	32	24	3	6	12	15	41	37
18.	Doncaster Rovers	42	10	7	4	28	17	4	2	15	23	54	37
19.	Nottingham Forest	42	8	8	5	43	22	4	3	14	26	54	35
20.	Barnsley	42	9	4	8	40	32	3	5	13	14	48	33
21.	Port Vale	42	10	5	6	34	30	2	3	16	22	76	32
22.	Hull City	42	4	7	10	33	45	1	3	17	14	66	20

Going Down 1936–37

United, the Division Two Champions in season 1935–36, slipped back into the Second Division after finishing in 21st place in Division One at the end of the 1936–37 season. However, United did manage to win the Manchester Senior Cup in 1936–37.

DID YOU KNOW THAT?
In a calamitous season, United also lost 5–0 at Arsenal in the fourth round of the FA Cup.

Football League Division 1 **1936–37**

		P	W	D	L	F	A	W	D	L	F	A	Pts
1.	Manchester City	42	15	5	1	56	22	7	8	6	51	39	57
2.	Charlton Athletic	42	15	5	1	37	13	6	7	8	21	36	54
3.	Arsenal	42	10	10	1	43	20	8	6	7	37	29	52
4.	Derby County	42	13	3	5	58	39	8	4	9	38	51	49
5.	Wolverhampton W	42	16	2	3	63	24	5	3	13	21	43	47
6.	Brentford	42	14	5	2	58	32	4	5	12	24	46	46
7.	Middlesbrough	42	14	6	1	49	22	5	2	14	25	49	46
8.	Sunderland	42	17	2	2	59	24	2	4	15	30	63	44
9.	Portsmouth	42	13	3	5	41	29	4	7	10	21	37	44
10.	Stoke City	42	12	6	3	52	27	3	6	12	20	30	42
11.	Birmingham City	42	9	7	5	36	24	4	8	9	28	36	41
12.	Grimsby Town	42	13	3	5	60	32	4	4	13	26	49	41
13.	Chelsea	42	11	6	4	36	21	3	7	11	16	34	41
14.	Preston North End	42	10	6	5	35	28	4	7	10	21	39	41
15.	Huddersfield Town	42	12	5	4	39	21	0	10	11	23	43	39
16.	WBA	42	13	3	5	45	32	3	3	15	32	66	38
17.	Everton	42	12	7	2	56	23	2	2	17	25	55	37
18.	Liverpool	42	9	8	4	38	26	3	3	15	24	58	35
19.	Leeds United	42	14	3	4	44	20	1	1	19	16	60	34
20.	Bolton Wanderers	42	6	6	9	22	33	4	8	9	21	33	34
21.	**Manchester United**	**42**	**8**	**9**	**4**	**29**	**26**	**2**	**3**	**16**	**26**	**52**	**32**
22.	Sheffield Wednesday	42	8	5	8	32	29	1	7	13	21	40	30

Going Up 1937–38

After winning the Division Two Championship in 1935–36, then suffering relegation back to Division Two in 1936–37, United were promoted to Division One for the second time in three seasons after finishing in runners-up spot in Division Two at the end of the 1937–38 season. United also won the Lancashire Senior Cup in 1937–38.

DID YOU KNOW THAT?
Jack Rowley and Stan Pearson both made their club debuts.

Football League Division 2 **1937–38**

		P	W	D	L	F	A	W	D	L	F	A	Pts
1.	Aston Villa	42	17	2	2	50	12	8	5	8	23	23	57
2.	**Manchester United**	**42**	**15**	**3**	**3**	**50**	**18**	**7**	**6**	**8**	**32**	**32**	**53**
3.	Sheffield United	42	15	4	2	46	19	7	5	9	27	37	53
4.	Coventry City	42	12	5	4	31	15	8	7	6	35	30	52
5.	Tottenham Hotspur	42	14	3	4	46	16	5	3	13	30	38	44
6.	Burnley	42	15	4	2	35	11	2	6	13	19	43	44
7.	Bradford Park Ave	42	13	4	4	51	22	4	5	12	18	34	43
8.	Fulham	42	10	7	4	44	23	6	4	11	17	34	43
9.	West Ham United	42	13	5	3	34	16	1	9	11	19	36	42
10.	Bury	42	12	3	6	43	26	6	2	13	20	34	41
11.	Chesterfield	42	12	2	7	39	24	4	7	10	24	39	41
12.	Luton Town	42	10	6	5	53	36	5	4	12	36	50	40
13.	Plymouth Argyle	42	10	7	4	40	30	4	5	12	17	35	40
14.	Norwich City	42	11	5	5	35	28	3	6	12	21	47	39
15.	Southampton	42	12	6	3	42	26	3	3	15	13	51	39
16.	Blackburn Rovers	42	13	6	2	51	30	1	4	16	20	50	38
17.	Sheffield Wednesday	42	10	5	6	27	21	4	5	12	22	35	38
18.	Swansea Town	42	12	6	3	31	21	1	6	14	14	52	38
19.	Newcastle United	42	12	4	5	38	18	2	4	15	13	40	36
20.	Nottingham Forest	42	12	3	6	29	21	2	5	14	18	39	36
21.	Barnsley	42	7	11	3	30	20	4	3	14	20	44	36
22.	Stockport County	42	8	6	7	24	24	3	3	15	19	46	31

Going Down 1973–74

In their final League game of the 1973–74 season United lost 1–0 at Stoke City and were relegated to Division 2. The side recorded only ten League wins out of 42 – the club's post-war record low, while their 20 League defeats was the most in the post-war era. Remarkably every Manchester United player, numbered 1 to 12, scored during the season.

DID YOU KNOW THAT?
Goalkeeper Alex Stepney converted two penalties in 1973–74.

Football League Division 1 **1973–74**

		P	W	D	L	F	A	W	D	L	F	A	Pts
1.	Leeds United	42	12	8	1	38	18	12	6	3	28	13	62
2.	Liverpool	42	18	2	1	34	11	4	11	6	18	20	57
3.	Derby County	42	13	7	1	40	16	4	7	10	12	26	48
4.	Ipswich Town	42	10	7	4	38	21	8	4	9	29	37	47
5.	Stoke City	42	13	6	2	39	15	2	10	9	15	27	46
6.	Burnley	42	10	9	2	29	16	6	5	10	27	37	46
7.	Everton	42	12	7	2	29	14	4	5	12	21	34	44
8.	QPR	42	8	10	3	30	17	5	7	9	26	35	43
9.	Leicester City	42	10	7	4	35	17	3	9	9	16	24	42
10.	Arsenal	42	9	7	5	23	16	5	7	9	26	35	42
11.	Tottenham Hotspur	42	9	4	8	26	27	5	10	6	19	23	42
12.	Wolverhampton W	42	11	6	4	30	18	2	9	10	19	31	41
13.	Sheffield United	42	7	7	7	25	22	7	5	9	19	27	40
14.	Manchester City	42	10	7	4	25	17	4	5	12	14	29	40
15.	Newcastle United	42	9	6	6	28	21	4	6	11	21	27	38
16.	Coventry City	42	10	5	6	25	18	4	5	12	18	36	38
17.	Chelsea	42	9	4	8	36	29	3	9	9	20	31	37
18.	West Ham United	42	7	7	7	36	32	4	8	9	19	28	37
19.	Birmingham City	42	10	7	4	30	21	2	6	13	22	43	37
20.	Southampton	42	8	10	3	30	20	3	4	14	17	48	36
21.	**Manchester United**	**42**	**7**	**7**	**7**	**23**	**20**	**3**	**5**	**13**	**15**	**28**	**32**
22.	Norwich City	42	6	9	6	25	27	1	6	14	12	35	29

Going Up 1974–75

In the final League game of the 1974–75 season United crushed Blackpool 4–0 at Old Trafford (Stuart Pearson 2, Brian Greenhoff, Lou Macari) to claim their second Division 2 championship. United were back in Division 1 after a one-year absence.

DID YOU KNOW THAT?
Aston Villa came runners-up to United in the Premier League in 1992–93, and amazingly Norwich City again finished third.

Football League Division 2 **1974–75**

		P	W	D	L	F	A	W	D	L	F	A	Pts
1.	**Manchester United**	42	17	3	1	45	12	9	6	6	21	18	61
2.	Aston Villa	42	16	4	1	47	6	9	4	8	32	26	58
3.	Norwich City	42	14	3	4	34	17	6	10	5	24	20	53
4.	Sunderland	42	14	6	1	41	8	5	7	9	24	27	51
5.	Bristol City	42	14	5	2	31	10	7	3	11	16	23	50
6.	WBA	42	13	4	4	33	15	5	5	11	21	27	45
7.	Blackpool	42	12	6	3	31	17	2	11	8	7	16	45
8.	Hull City	42	12	8	1	25	10	3	6	12	15	43	44
9.	Fulham	42	9	8	4	29	17	4	8	9	15	22	42
10.	Bolton Wanderers	42	9	7	5	27	16	6	5	10	18	25	42
11.	Oxford United	42	14	3	4	30	19	1	9	11	11	32	42
12.	Leyton Orient	42	8	9	4	17	16	3	11	7	11	23	42
13.	Southampton	42	10	6	5	29	20	5	5	11	24	34	41
14.	Notts County	42	7	11	3	34	26	5	5	11	15	33	40
15.	York City	42	9	7	5	28	18	5	3	13	23	37	38
16.	Nottingham Forest	42	7	7	7	24	23	5	7	9	19	32	38
17.	Portsmouth	42	9	5	5	28	20	3	6	12	16	34	37
18.	Oldham Athletic	42	10	7	4	28	16	0	8	13	12	32	35
19.	Bristol Rovers	42	10	4	7	25	23	2	7	12	17	41	35
20.	Millwall	42	8	9	4	31	19	2	3	16	13	37	32
21.	Cardiff City	42	7	8	6	24	21	2	6	13	12	41	32
22.	Sheffield Wednesday	42	3	7	11	17	29	2	4	15	12	35	21

MANCHESTER UNITED QUIZ

We all know that Manchester United has been the most successful club in England over the past 20 years and, in the previous pages, you have relived many of the greatest moments in the glorious history of the Reds.

But how much do you really know about United, their players, managers, opponents and events? On the following pages are 10 quizzes, each with 20 questions, all to do with the Reds. Some are specialist and others are Pot Luck.

For some fans, every question will be as easy as a Wayne Rooney tap-in, for others the questions will be very tough. But don't worry, and to make things easier, in many cases, the answer will have appeared elsewhere in the book as part of a different story. Rest assured, there are no trick questions, no fiendish cryptic clues to melt your brain, just simple memory or general knowledge questions.

The style of the quizzes is such that you can set up your own United pub quiz night or pass a long car, train or plane journey to a Reds game. All you would need are some pens and paper (but it's best not to get the car driver involved if the answers are going to be written down) and you're ready go.

Oh yes, to show we are very nice people, we have provided all the answers at the end of the section so you can check to see how you have done.

Quiz 1: Pot Luck 1

1   What is the name of the road which runs past the front entrance of Old Trafford?
2   Which goalkeeper joined United from Fulham in 2005?
3   What is the nationality of former United brothers Rafael and Fabio?
4   Which United player captained England at the 2002 World Cup?
5   Who was the 2010 Football Writers Footballer of the Year?
6   Against which of his former clubs did Sir Alex Ferguson manage in the 2010/11 Champions League?
7   Who was named in the England World Cup 2010 finals squad but withdrew because of injury?
8   Which United legend missed three penalties for the club in 1968–69?
9   To the nearest thousand, what was the attendance in the match when United played in front of the biggest crowd in Football League history?
10 Who did United sign from Blackburn Rovers in June 2011?
11 Who was penalty shoot-out hero in the 2009 Carling Cup final victory over Tottenham Hotspur?
12 In which season did United achieve their record Premier League points total of 92?
13 Which sport held its Super League Grand Final at Old Trafford in 2010?
14 How old was Sir Alex Ferguson when he celebrated his birthday on 31 December 2010?
15 In which country was Owen Hargreaves born?
16 For which Spanish club did Jordi Cruyff win a UEFA Cup runners-up medal in 2001?
17 Which former United striker scored a hat-trick for Northern Ireland against Spain in 2006?
18 England international striker Garry Birtles waited 30 matches for his first League goal for United. True or false?
19 Which United striker was the first player to score five goals in a Premier League match?
20 Who replaced Frank O'Farrell as United boss in December 1972?

Quiz 2: Ryan Giggs

1   In which city was Ryan Giggs born?
2   What was Ryan's surname before he changed it to Giggs?
3   Ryan attended which club's School of Excellence from 1985 to 1987?
4   Against which opponents did Ryan make his senior debut in March 1991?
5   Who was the boss who gave Giggs his international debut?
6   What winner's medal did Ryan collect at the end of his first season as a United regular?
7   How many FA Cup winner's medals has Giggs won?
8   How did Ryan celebrate his 1999 FA Cup semi-final replay winner against Arsenal?
9   When did Ryan win the BBC Sports Personality of the Year award?
10 What is Ryan's middle name?
11 Who did United beat when Ryan won the 1992 FA Youth Cup?
12 How many times has Ryan netted in an FA Cup Final?
13 Which two long-time team-mates also have made 600 appearances for the Reds?
14 How many games was Ryan in charge of the first team for after the sacking of David Moyes in April 2014?
15 What is the name of Ryan's younger brother?
16 When did Giggs win his second PFA Young Player of the Year award?
17 In which match and against whom did Ryan break United's all-time club appearance record?
18 How many Premier League champions medals does Ryan own?
19 In which year did Ryan marry Stacey Cooke?
20 In August 2010, against which club did Ryan Giggs become the first player to score in the first 19 seasons of the Premier League?

Quiz 3: Sir Alex Ferguson

1   Who did Alex Ferguson succeed as Manchester United manager?
2   In which month and year did Fergie take the reins at Old Trafford?
3   When Ferguson was appointed manager at United, which of his former Aberdeen stars was already at Old Trafford?
4   What was Alex's first match with United?
5   Which England full-back was Alex's first purchase, from Arsenal in July 1987?
6   By what nickname was Alex's early and young United squad known?
7   Which of Sir Alex's sons became a manager in the Championship in 2009?
8   What was United's first major trophy success under Alex?
9   Which United chairman appointed Alex Ferguson?
10 Which former Fergie assistant went on to become England manager in 2006?
11 What is the name of the most successful racehorse owned by Sir Alex?
12 In what year did Fergie become Sir Alex?
13 Where was Alex when he found out that United were champions in 1992–93?
14 Who, in August 1995, told the football world in general, and Fergie in particular, that 'you win nothing with kids'?
15 Who would have 'loved it, really loved it' if Fergie's team had been beaten to the title by Newcastle in 1995–96?
16 How many more top-flight titles did United win under Sir Alex than they won prior to his arrival?
17 Against which club has Fergie won and lost European finals?
18 Which of Sir Alex's former assistants was sacked as Portugal coach in 2010?
19 What was the score when United played City at Old Trafford in September 2009?
20 Sir Alex is the father of how many sons?

Quiz 4: Pot Luck 2

1   Which inter-war United half-back became England's first and longest-serving manager?

2   Which Irish winger scored on his senior United debut in an FA Cup tie with Bury in January 1993?

3   Bobby Charlton was United's top League scorer in 1972–73, his last term as a United player, with how many goals?

4   From which London club did United sign Reg Allen, the keeper who helped to lift the League title in 1951–52?

5   In May 2001 United played a so-called 'Battle of Britain' testimonial match against which club?

6   Who became chairman of Manchester United in 1980?

7   Who did United play at Old Trafford in August 1978 to celebrate the centenary of Newton Heath's foundation?

8   United played in front of the highest attendance in Football League history. On what ground did that game take place?

9   Who scored the opening goal in the 2017 Europa League final?

10 For which cricketer did United play a testimonial at Scunthorpe in 1984?

11 What was United's lowest post-war points total, compiled when they were relegated in 1973–74?

12 How many Premiership goals did United score in 1999–2000?

13 Of which ex United Dutchman, did Martin Buchan once say: 'He's the only man in English football I would pay to watch'?

14 Which ex-United striker was Huddersfield Town boss in 2007–08?

15 Which youth coach nurtured the class of 1992, featuring Beckham, Scholes, Butt and the Neville brothers?

16 Which former United keeper was the USA's No. 1 at the 2010 World Cup?

17 Against which club did Dimitar Berbatov score a September 2010 Premiership hat-trick?

18 Where did United finish in the 2016–17 Premier League season?

19 Albert Kinsey scored twice in an FA Cup tie against Chester in January 1965, his only senior outing for United. True or false?

20 Who scored for United in the 2011 Champions League final?

Quiz 5: Jose Mourinho

United coach Jose Mourinho has enjoyed great success where ever he has been in charge, but how much do you know about his career?

1   In what position did Jose play during his playing career?

2   Jose's first club as a coach met United in the 1968 European Cup Final. Who are they?

3   How many clubs did Jose coach before becoming United boss?

4   For which former England coach did Jose work at several clubs?

5   What was the first trophy he won as a manager?

6   Which club did Jose's FC Porto beat in the 2003 UEFA Cup final?

7   Who succeeded Jose as the coach of Inter Milan?

8   Who scored twice in the 2003 UEFA Cup final and later joined United?

9   At which club did he achieve his highest win ratio of 71.9%?

10 Jose enjoyed a run of 150 home league matches undefeated between 2002 and 2011, but at which clubs was he coach?

11 How many league titles did Jose win between 2000 and 2017

12 What was the first trophy he won with Chelsea?

13 How many times has he won the Onze d'Or Coach of the Year?

14 Which trophy did United win for the first time under Mourinho?

15 Which Portuguese coach has worked with Jose since 2002?

16 Who did Jose succeed as the Coach of Real Madrid?

17 In what seasons did he win the Premier League title at Chelsea?

18 Which Dutch Barcelona coach did Jose have a row with in 2005?

19 How many times has he won the FIFA World Coach of the Year?

20 Who was the first player Jose signed for Manchester United?

Quiz 6: They said it

Who said the following;

1 "Football, eh, bloody hell!"
2 "When the seagulls follow the trawler it is because they think sardines will be thrown into the sea."
3 "Winning isn't everything. There should be no conceit in victory and no despair in defeat."
4 "I don't know about professional referees. They love themselves enough as it is now."
5 "I think I've found a genius."
6 "I went for the ball, that was all I could see, it was definitely playable."
7 "Bloody hell, this United team could win the Boat Race."
8 "I'm a footballer. But I'm also a company."
9 "I see myself as a fan who plays for the team."
10 "To become Manchester United manager is a special honour. There is a mystique and a romance about it which no other club can match."
11 "I have a prawn sandwich every now and then myself."
12 "Loyalty has been the anchor of my life and it's something I learned in Govan."
13 "I am a lion. I don't want to be a lion."
14 "Nobby Stiles doesn't so much tackle people as bump into them."
15 "I gave them the Cup and they gave me the sack."
16 "I have no time for longevity. Living fast and hard, that's what interests me."
17 "What do they want me to do? Go out and smash up some bar?"
18 "Maybe in the future I could return."
19 "When an Italian tells me it's pasta on the plate, I check under the sauce to make sure."
20 "I have been here since I was a young boy and I have grown very fond of the club and the fans."

Quiz 7: Pot Luck 3

1   From which club did United sign Dimitar Berbatov in 2009?
2   Which United and England star decided not to come out of international retirement for the 2010 World Cup?
3   Who had the squad number 19 for United in 2016–17?
4   Sir Alex Ferguson was the first Scotsman to receive a knighthood for his services to football. True or false?
5   In which country did United win their third UEFA Champions League/European Cup trophy?
6   Which United assistant manager and ex-player won his only England cap in 1989?
7   Against which club did Wayne Rooney score a United debut hat-trick in 2004?
8   Who was United's second-choice keeper at the start of 2010–11?
9   Who was the last man to earn 50 Scotland caps, all while a United player?
10 What was the score in the 2008 Champions League final penalty shoot-out?
11 Which United player was named FIFA World Player of the Year in 2008?
12 Which Essex club has never lost to United and beat them in the 2006 Carling Cup?
13 Which 1990s United player was nicknamed "Choccy"?
14 Which country did Dwight Yorke represent?
15 In which year did United win the Champions League, League and FA Cup treble?
16 Who was United's last English-born Football Writers' Footballer of the Year?
17 In which year did United mark the 50th anniversary of the Munich Air Disaster?
18 Who scored United's winner in the April 2010 Manchester derby?
19 What was the score when United ended Arsenal's 49-game unbeaten run in 2004?
20 Solve the anagram: I CARPET VERA.

Quiz 8: The Neville brothers

1   Which Neville has a twin sister, Tracey, a netball international?
2   How many League appearances did Phil make for United before joining Everton?
3   Which Neville played the full 90 minutes of the 1996 FA Cup Final?
4   Who did the other Neville brother replace near the end of the 1996 FA Cup Final?
5   Neville Neville, Gary & Philip's father, was commercial manager at which club?
6   In which year did Gary captain United to victory in the FA Youth Cup?
7   Which future England captain played with Phil in Lancashire's U-19 cricket team?
8   How many goals did Gary score for United during his career?
9   What is Phil's date of birth?
10 In which cathedral did Gary marry Emma Hadfield in June 2007?
11 Which Neville was selected for the PFA Premiership team in four successive seasons from 1995/96 to 1998/99?
12 Phil made his senior United debut in the FA Cup, against which opponents?
13 In years, how old was Phil when he won his first full England cap?
14 In which year did Phil leave United?
15 Who were the opponents when Gary made his United debut in September 1992?
16 In which year did Gary win his first full England cap?
17 How often did Gary and Phil start in the same England team?
18 Which brother was a last-minute omission from England's party for the 1998 World Cup Finals?
19 When did Phil emulate Gary and lead United to FA Youth Cup glory?
20 Gary's first League goal came against which opponents in the 1996–97 season?

Quiz 9: Birthday boys

Which United legends were born on this day and in this place?

1   18 February 1975, Bury.
2   15 May 1977, Leytonstone, London.
3   10 August 1971, Cork, Republic of Ireland.
4   26 May 1909, Belshill, Scotland.
5   24 February 1940, Aberdeen, Scotland.
6   5 February 1985, Funchal, Madeira.
7   30 January 1981, Blagoevgrad, Bulgaria.
8   16 November 1974, Salford.
9   7 November 1978, Peckham, London.
10   1 November 1963, Wrexham, Wales.
11   11 October 1937, Ashington, Tyne & Wear.
12   18 May 1942, Manchester.
13   18 November 1963, Gladsaxe, Denmark.
14   11 January 1957, Chester-le-Street, Durham.
15   4 December 1959, Ealing, London.
16   30 July 1874, Chirk, Wales.
17   24 May 1966, Marseille, France.
18   27 May 1971, Halesowen, West Midlands.
19   1 October 1936, Dudley, West Midlands.
20   1 July 1976, North Brabant, Netherlands.

Quiz 10: Pot Luck 4

1   What is the translation of Mexican star Javier "Chicarito" Hernandez's nickname?
2   From which club did United sign Nemanja Vidic?
3   Which two United brothers played for Northern Ireland in 2010?
4   By what score did United beat Leicester City to win the 2016 FA Community Shield?
5   Which ex-United legend became Stoke City boss in 2013?
6   Who did Manchester United ground-share with while Old Trafford was rebuilt in the 1940s?
7   Whose United appearance record was passed by Ryan Giggs in 2008?
8   Who made his United debut against Leeds in May 1998 aged 18?
9   How many times have United won three consecutive Premier League titles?
10 Which former United defender has managed the likes of Birmingham, Wigan, Sunderland and Aston Villa?
11 Which of Bobby Charlton's United team-mates played in the 1966 World Cup final?
12 Which former Celtic star joined United from Helsingborg on loan in 2007?
13 Who was the last man to be a regular United first-teamer aged 40?
14 Who was the Champions League top scorer in 2007–08?
15 True or false: United retained the Carling Cup in 2010 beating Aston Villa in the final.
16 Which London team lost 3–0 to Manchester United in the 2004 FA Cup final?
17 Is the trident to the right or left of the Red Devil on the club badge?
18 Whose statue, unveiled in 1996, stands outside Old Trafford?
19 In which year did Manchester United first play at Old Trafford?
20 Solve this anagram: AY NEW ONE ROY.

Answers

QUIZ 1 – Pot Luck 1

1 Sir Matt Busby Way. **2** Edwin van der Sar. **3** Brazilian. **4** David Beckham.
5 Wayne Rooney. **6** Rangers. **7** Rio Ferdinand. **8** Denis Law. **9** 82,000.
10 Phil Jones. **11** Ben Foster. **12** 1993–94. **13** Rugby League. **14** 69.
15 Canada. **16** RCD Alaves. **17** David Healy. **18** True. **19** Andrew Cole.
20 Tommy Docherty.

QUIZ 2 – Ryan Giggs

1 Cardiff. **2** Wilson. **3** Manchester City. **4** Everton. **5** Terry Yorath.
6 League Cup. **7** Four. **8** He tore off his shirt and waved it round his head.
9 2009. **10** Joseph. **11** Crystal Palace. **12** None. **13** Paul Scholes and
Gary Neville. **14** Four – W2, L1, D1. **15** Rhodri. **16** 1993. **17** Chelsea, 2008
UEFA Champions League Final. **18** 13. **19** 2007. **20** Newcastle United.

QUIZ 3 – Sir Alex Ferguson

1 Ron Atkinson. **2** November 1986. **3** Gordon Strachan. **4** Away to Oxford
United. **5** Viv Anderson. **6** Fergie's Fledglings. **7** Darren. **8** The FA Cup in
1990. **9** Martin Edwards. **10** Steve McClaren. **11** Rock of Gibraltar.
12 1999. **13** On a golf course. **14** Alan Hansen. **15** Kevin Keegan. **16** Six.
17 FC Barcelona. **18** Carlos Queiroz. **19** United 2, City 3. **20** Three.

QUIZ 4 – Pot Luck 2

1 Walter Winterbottom. **2** Keith Gillespie. **3** Six. **4** QPR. **5** Celtic.
6 Martin Edwards. **7** Real Madrid. **8** Maine Road. **9** Paul Pogba.
10 Ian Botham. **11** 32 points. **12** 97 goals. **13** Arnold Muhren.
14 Andy Ritchie. **15** Eric Harrison. **16** Tim Howard. **17** Liverpool.
18 Sixth. **19** False, he scored once. George Best scored the other.
20 Wayne Rooney.

QUIZ 5 – Jose Mourinho

1 Midfield. **2** Benfica. **3** Six (Benfica, Leiria, Porto, Chelsea [twice], Inter Milan
and Real Madrid). **4** Sir Bobby Robson. **5** Primeira Liga in Portugal. **6** Celtic,
3–2 aet. **7** Rafael Benitez. **8** Henrik Larsson. **9** Real Madrid. **10** Porto (W36,
D2), Chelsea (W46, D16), Inter Milan (W29, D9) and Real Madrid (W14, D0).
11 Eight (Porto two, Chelsea 3, Inter Milan 2, Real Madrid 1). **12** League Cup.
13 Once (Chelsea, 2005). **14** UEFA Europa League (in 2017). **15** Rui Faria.
16 Manuel Pellegrini. **17** 2004–05, 2005–06, 2014–15. **18** Frank Rijkaard.
19 Once (Inter Milan, 2010). **20** Eric Bailly from Villareal.

QUIZ 6 – They said it

1 Sir Alex Ferguson. **2** Eric Cantona. **3** Sir Matt Busby. **4** Paul Scholes.
5 Bob Bishop, who discovered George Best. **6** Kevin Moran, after being
sent off in the FA Cup Final. **7** Bill Shankly. **8** Peter Schmeichel. **9** David
Beckham. **10** Jose Mourinho. **11** Roy Keane. **12** Sir Alex Ferguson.
13 Zlatan Ibrahimovic. **14** Bobby Charlton. **15** Tommy Docherty.
16 Eric Cantona. **17** Gary Neville. **18** Cristiano Ronaldo. **19** Sir Alex
Ferguson. **20** Ryan Giggs.

QUIZ 7 – Pot Luck 3

1 Tottenham Hotspur. **2** Paul Scholes. **3** Marcus Rashford. **4** False, Sir
Matt Busby was first. **5** Russia. **6** Mike Phelan. **7** Fenerbahce. **8** Tomasz
Kuszczak. **9** Darren Fletcher. **10** United 6, Chelsea 5. **11** Cristiano Ronaldo.
12 Southend United. **13** Brian McClair. **14** Trinidad & Tobago. **15** 1999.
16 Wayne Rooney, 2010. **17** 2008. **18** Paul Scholes. **19** 2–0.
20 Patrice Evra.

QUIZ 8 – The Neville brothers

1 Phil. **2** 263. **3** Phil. **4** David Beckham. **5** Bury. **6** 1992. **7** Andrew
Flintoff. **8** Seven. **9** 21 January 1977. **10** Manchester. **11** Gary.
12 Wrexham. **13** 19 years old. **14** 2005. **15** Torpedo Moscow.
16 1995. **17** 31. **18** Phil. **19** 1995. **20** Middlesbrough.

QUIZ 9 – Birthday boys

1 Gary Neville. **2** David Beckham. **3** Roy Keane. **4** Sir Matt Busby.
5 Denis Law. **6** Cristiano Ronaldo. **7** Dimitar Berbatov. **8** Paul Scholes.
9 Rio Ferdinand. **10** Mark Hughes. **11** Sir Bobby Charlton. **12** Nobby
Stiles. **13** Peter Schmeichel. **14** Bryan Robson. **15** Paul McGrath.
16 Billy Meredith. **17** Eric Cantona. **18** Lee Sharpe. **19** Duncan Edwards.
20 Ruud van Nistelrooy.

QUIZ 10 – Pot Luck 4

1 Little pea. **2** Spartak Moscow. **3** Jonny and Corry Evans. **4** 2–1.
5 Mark Hughes. **6** Manchester City. **7** Sir Bobby Charlton. **8** Wes Brown.
9 Twice. **10** Steve Bruce. **11** Nobby Stiles. **12** Henrik Larsson.
13 Edwin van der Sar. **14** Cristiano Ronaldo. **15** True. **16** Millwall.
17 Right. **18** Sir Matt Busby. **19** 1910. **20** Wayne Rooney.

PICTURE QUIZ 1: NO PLACE LIKE HOME
A Bank Street, Manchester; **B** Old Trafford, Manchester; **C** Maine Road, Manchester; **D** Home Park, Plymouth.

PICTURE QUIZ 2: READER, I MARRIED HIM
A Angie Best (née MacDonald) – George Best; **B** Coleen Rooney (née McLoughlin) – Wayne Rooney; **C** Helena Seger – Zlatan Ibrahimovic; **D** Victoria Beckham (née Adams, aka Posh Spice) – David Beckham.

PICTURE QUIZ 3: THE APPRENTICE
A Louis van Gaal; **B** Dave Sexton; **C** Ron Atkinson; **D** Alex Ferguson.

PICTURE QUIZ 4: BAD HAIR DAY
A Bobby Charlton; **B** Marouane Fellaini; **C** David Beckham; **D** John Fitzpatrick.

PICTURE QUIZ 5: ERIC'S OEUVRE
A Looking For Eric; **B** The Over-Eater; **C** French Film; **D** The Second Wind.

PICTURE QUIZ 6: MYSTERY MEN AT THE EUROS
A Anthony Martial (France); **B** Wayne Rooney (England); **C** Paddy McNair (Northern Ireland); **D** David De Gea (Spain).

PICTURE QUIZ 7: REMIND YOU OF ANYBODY?
A Zeus (Zlatan Ibrahimovic – self-proclaimed "God of Old Trafford"); **B** Hair dryer (Sir Alex Ferguson); **C** Prawn sandwich (Roy Keane); **D** Eric Cantona (seagulls).

PICTURE QUIZ 8: WEAR IT WITH PRIDE
A 1992–93 (Lee Sharpe); **B** 1975–76 (Lou Macari); **C** 1990–91 (Ryan Giggs); **D** 2001–02 (Phil Neville).